Sunday Morning Quilts

16 Modern Scrap Projects

Sort, Store, and Use Every Last Bit of Your Treasured Fabrics

Amanda Jean Nyberg

and

Cheryl Arkison

stashBOOKS.

an imprint of C&T Publishing

Text and Photography copyright © 2012 by Amanda Jean Nyberg and Cheryl Arkison

Photography and Artwork copyright © 2012 by C&T Publishing, Inc.

Publisher: Amy Marson

Creative Director: Gailen Runge

Acquisitions Editor: Susanne Woods

Editor: Lynn Koolish

Technical Editors: Mary E. Flynn
and Gailen Runge

Cover/Book Designer: Kristy Zacharias

Production Coordinator: Zinnia Heinzmann

Production Editors: Alice Mace Nakanishi
and S. Michele Fry

Illustrator: Mary E. Flynn

Flat Quilt and Style Photography by
Christina Carty-Francis and Diane Pedersen of
C&T Publishing, Inc.; How-To Photography by
Amanda Jean Nyberg and Cheryl Arkison, unless
otherwise noted

Published by Stash Books, an imprint of C&T Publishing, Inc., P.O. Box 1456, Lafayette, CA 94549

Library of Congress Cataloging-in-Publication Data

Nyberg, Amanda Jean, 1975-

 Sunday morning quilts : 16 modern scrap projects : sort, store, and use every last bit of your treasured
fabrics / Amanda Jean Nyberg and Cheryl Arkison.

     p. cm.

 ISBN 978-1-60705-427-6 (soft cover)

1. Patchwork--Patterns. 2. Quilting--Patterns. I. Arkison, Cheryl, 1975- II. Title.

 TT835.N93 2012

 746.46--dc23

                    2011034028

Printed in China

10 9 8 7 6 5 4 3

Dedications

FROM CHERYL

For Baba, Nettie Ciona, who I think would have been proud of this (even if her definition of success meant working in an office). May my house be as filled with quilts as hers was with cross-stitch.

FROM AMANDA JEAN

I would like to dedicate this book to Nancy March, the wonderful woman who taught me how to quilt.

Acknowledgments

From Cheryl

Without a doubt, this book wouldn't exist without two people. First, my husband, Morgan Arkison. His unflinching support and pushes along the way are a testament to his being the bestest husband ever.

Second, without Amanda Jean this project never would have happened. This was a true creative collaboration from concept to completion.

I can't forget the whole host of characters in my life who encourage (or at least tolerate) this passion of mine. My kids, whose hands pulled threads or pushed the foot pedal on many a project. My immediate family, who did everything, including watch the kids, test patterns, and call me when I needed to be working, and tried not to be too shocked when I quit my desk job to be a quilter and writer. My friends who don't quite understand this passion of mine—I'm thankful you keep me from being too much of a nerd.

From Amanda Jean

I would like to thank God, my creator, who has given me the ability to create.

I would like to thank my husband for being ever so supportive throughout this whole process. Thank you for believing in me, for helping me step out of my comfort zone, and for being beside me every step of the way. Thank you, from the bottom of my heart.

Thanks to my wonderful kids, who understood when I said, "Not right now—Mom's working." You are the best kids any mama could ask for.

Thanks to my extended family and friends for being there for me and for helping me along the way. Your encouragement made all the difference. I could not have done this without your support!

Last but not least, thank you to Cheryl, my co-author and friend. I'm so happy that we teamed up to do this.

From Both of Us

Thanks to Stash Books for the opportunity to bring our scraps to the world. Thank you to Susanne Woods, Lynn Koolish, and the entire staff at C&T. A special thank-you to Diane Pedersen, who went above and beyond by answering our 101 photo questions. Thanks, Diane, for your patience and guidance as we worked through this project!

Thanks to the folks who contributed their own scraps and fabric to the cause: Bernadette Kent at Traditional Pastimes, Beth Schmidt, Jacquie Gering, Jan DiCinto, Natashia Ciona, Marisa Haedike, Pat Sloan, Clair Wolters, Laura Conaway, Beth Bitts, Terri Wilhelm, Heather Bechtold, Carolyn Strug, and all the blog friends who have shared their scraps with us throughout the years.

Thanks to the folks who tested our patterns: Jennifer Bailey, Natashia Ciona, Pauline Francis, Katherine Greaves, Wanda Hanson, Meredith Helgeson, Andrea Homer-Macdonald, Pam Lincoln, Tara Rebman, Barbara Robson, Lesley Wade-Woolley, and Terri Wilhelm. Thanks to Susan Lutjen O'Connor for brilliantly naming *The Original Ticker Tape* and *Splash* quilts.

Finally, thank you to the readers and friends we've shared our lives with through our blogs. It is thanks to your cheerleading and encouragement that we continue to push ourselves creatively and bring our projects to the world. You also keep us honest and humble. Thank you.

Contents

Scrap Sorting and Storage

Quilt Construction Basics

The Projects

Introduction

As long as there are quilts there will be scraps. As long as there are scraps there will be scrap quilts.

With the proliferation of new, bright, and modern designer fabrics, many quilters are left with fabric so precious to them that they are hanging on to every last inch. With the modern quilt movement growing, in terms of both fabrics and techniques, modern quilters need options for sorting, storing, and using their scraps effectively and beautifully.

Making quilts from your scraps is partly about embracing the frugal history of quiltmaking. Long before there were stores devoted to quilting cottons, there were the leftovers from home-sewn clothes, linens, and cloth feedsacks. Buying fabric just for quilts was sometimes a luxury. Many quilts were made with what was available rather than what was wanted.

In the modern age, when new fabric is easily at hand and overwhelmingly inspiring, it's easy to put the scraps aside and move on to the next project and the next group of fabrics. Just because we are modern quilters, we shouldn't forget those traditional roots. Nor can we ignore the waste if we just throw out the scraps.

Scrap quilting is about celebrating gorgeous fabric. It is about making something amazing out of the odds and ends that are causing havoc in our sewing space. It is about being mindful of what we have. It is about pushing our creative limits to find a way to utilize every last piece.

Sunday Morning Quilts marries the notion of the scrap quilt and modern quilt design. These quilts are bold, appealing to the new generation of quilters. They are at home in a modern setting—covering a platform bed, as an art installation, or on the back of a streamlined sofa. Better yet, wrapped around a pile of legs on the couch or used as the walls of a fort.

Ultimately, that's what it's all about—making a quilt to be used. We may love our fabric and thrill in the creative process, the best part is curling up with a quilt. Looking down from our mugs on a quiet morning to see the fabric from both our first and latest quilts is satisfying, and we encourage you to take your scraps out and make your own Sunday morning quilts.

OUR JOURNEY TO THE SCRAP PILE

Combined, we have almost as many years of quilting experience as we are old! We've made more than 250 quilts. As you can imagine, we have a lot of scraps. *A lot.*

We came together through the power of the Internet. Okay, that's giving a lot of credit to the Internet. Beyond our blogs, we're both busy moms with a tendency to go crazy over clutter and to drown in our fabric. We share ideas and help each other out when we're stuck on a quilt or life in general. This book emerged out of those conversations.

We aren't the same type of quilter. Our fabric preferences vary, our goals are different, and the rate at which we work is light years apart. But we do come together when we talk about scraps. There comes a point when they take over your space, your life, and your inspiration. If they aren't dealt with *right now* then nothing else can be done. We totally get that about each other.

Scrap quilting isn't new to us, or to anyone. We wanted to make quilts that we loved making and using. And we wanted to deal with every last bit of fabric we had.

Could quilts be made with just *those little bits?* It turns out that the answer is a very obvious *YES!*

THIS BOOK

Sunday Morning Quilts is a direct response to that question. Stunning and bold quilts can be made with those little bits! And you can make a dent in the scrap pile while making those quilts.

The first step is effective sorting and storing of all your scraps. You can't get to the creating part without this step. In addition to strategies for sorting and storing, we've included a great project for storing those scraps—made from scraps! After that we've provided 15 inspirational designs to help you use up every last bit.

Not everyone will move through his or her scrap bin from one design to the next, but there is at least one quilt among all the designs

here that will get you running to your scraps, if not your stash.

We want to encourage you to make each quilt your own. Not only will your personal scrap selection inspire differences, but you can adapt the designs for the sizes and colors you want. Each project includes a few of our suggestions for design alternatives. We can't wait to see what you come up with.

This book is for the adventurous beginner, the experienced artist, and everyone in between. The techniques in *Sunday Morning Quilts* are easily adaptable for all quilters, so even the most traditional of quilters can take something from them. All we assume is that you have basic quilting skills and a pile of scraps begging for attention.

Even if you are a beginner and your scrap bin is actually rather empty, these designs are easily adapted to new fabric. You will just need to turn your fabric into scraps by chopping it up first. Or you can ask around to see if you can get your hands on someone else's scraps.

We've come a long way from our first quilts. But you know what? Those first fabrics are still around—and some of them are in these quilts. Embrace the roots of your quilting history and quilting in general. Take those scraps and move forward with these bold designs. You, and your fabric, will be very, very happy.

Define Modern

"simple yet
energetic
designs"

What Is Modern?

Our quilts are decidedly modern. A lot of factors combine to put them in the modern category. Design, construction, fabric choice, and color all influence whether a quilt is seen as modern. Perhaps what is most important, though, is how you see your quilts. Whether you see them as modern or not—or whether you are even concerned with that—being happy with your quilts at the end of the day is what matters most.

The modern quilt movement would not exist without the Internet. Blogging, photo sharing, community sites, and online shopping changed the face of quilting. Not only has the Internet opened up quilting to a younger audience, it's made for the quick and widespread sharing of ideas and concepts. With physical chapters of the Modern Quilt Guild now being established internationally, the online world is making a transition to in-person gatherings. It is a perfect metaphor for modern quilting as a whole.

Not much in modern quilting is radically new. We're still using fabric, thread, batting, and skill to put a quilt together. While some contemporary or art quilters love to include the use of paint, fusing, beads, paper, and more, modern quilters are actually more like traditional quilters in their choice of materials.

Modern quilts are also a lot like traditional quilts in their simplicity of design, use of solids, and color choices. Arguably, modern quilting could be considered a throwback to very, very traditional quilting.

It also has been argued that modern quilting is a mutation of current quilting conventions. As modern quilts are made, each new idea is tested and shared, and it continues to mutate. Every time you see a quilt, you can be sure that variations, adaptations, and new quilts will follow. Modern quilting takes traditional quilts and changes them, and it also takes contemporary quilts and steals their bold flavor.

The importance of history and tradition is acknowledged in modern quilting, but people often come to the movement either evolving from or rebelling against traditional or contemporary quilting.

Perhaps modern quilting is really a reflection of societal changes?

- Granddaughters looking to reclaim the skills of their grandmothers
- A push for domestic simplicity and a return to the craft of living
- Women (and a few men) acknowledging a creative outlet in a fast-paced, technology-driven world
- A younger batch of quilters looking for new inspiration
- A search for community beyond preschool and soccer games

These have resulted in the development of simple yet energetic designs—modern quilting.

Design

While no one factor makes a quilt modern, some design commonalities make modern quilts stand out from the rest of the stack.

LARGE SCALE

Regardless of the finished size of the quilt, the designs are often on a large scale. This can be manifested as a quilt that is one large block or a quilt made from a handful of large blocks. In a similar vein, modern quilts are often seen with large pieces of a single fabric. In part, this is a reflection of the desire to show off large-scale prints as well as a love for many modern fabrics.

CLEAN AND SIMPLE

Even when complex in construction, the designs of modern quilts are usually clean—it's like looking at an ultramodern home in comparison to a Victorian. Both houses serve the same purpose, but the design is radically different—the modern one is full of clean lines and spare spaces.

Modern quilters also have returned to basic shapes, such as squares, hexagons, circles, and half-square triangles. Intricately pieced blocks aren't commonly seen in modern quilting.

Stripes are also very popular.

NO BORDERS

It would be a generalization to say that there are no borders in modern quilts, but it isn't far from the truth.

NEGATIVE SPACE

Whether it is through the use of large bands of plain sashing between blocks or the appearance of blocks floating on the background, the use of negative space is prevalent in modern quilts. With so much blank space, there are many opportunities for the eyes to rest when looking at a modern quilt. These large blank areas also provide opportunities to showcase quilting stitches.

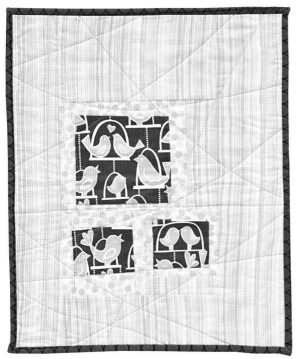

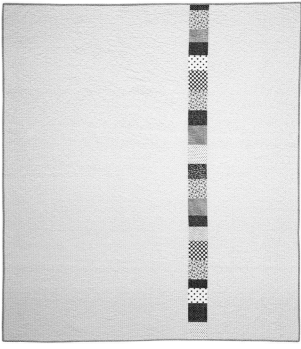

MADE BY CHERYL: Top left and bottom right
MADE BY AMANDA JEAN: Top right and bottom left

How It's Made

A modern quilt is put together like any other quilt: Place two pieces of fabric together and sew; add another piece and sew some more; repeat. That being said, certain construction techniques and the apparent absence of other techniques mark the majority of modern quilts.

WONKINESS / WABI SABI

Modern quilting embraces the imperfections of piecing and cutting. While the ¼″ seam still reigns, modern quilting doesn't always follow the strict guidelines of straight cuts and right angles. Most people call this wonkiness. In fact, a wonky Log Cabin may be the most popular modern block. Some people call this wabi sabi instead of wonkiness.

Wabi sabi is the notion of celebrating beauty in the slightly imperfect and the handmade. Some say that it also celebrates the passing of time that results in frayed edges, decay, and rust spots. Wabi sabi is also about discovering the quiet, the unexpected, the fragment in the beauty of a larger piece. Wabi sabi is not an excuse for poor work or not taking care.

IMPROVISATION

Although improvised piecing is certainly not new in the quilting world, it is predominant in modern quilting. This creates an emphasis on the process of quilting as much as on the finished product. At its most basic, this approach means you can throw all your pieces into a brown paper bag and sew the pieces together as you randomly pull out fabric. But it is more than that. Being able to improvise means working with what you've got, being okay when you run out of a particular fabric, or coming up with a creative solution when you are one block short.

BY HAND

Modern quilting shows no real preference for hand over machine, although most of us piece by machine these days. Appliqué is still around, but it isn't prevalent in this quilting style. Hand quilting, however, does still have a prominent place for many modern quilters. Unlike traditional quilting, however, modern hand stitching usually involves thicker thread and big stitches. Other handwork is growing in popularity, but patchwork still reigns.

MINIMAL FUSING

With the exception of some random appliqué, one thing not seen to any great extent in modern quilts is the use of fusible. Unlike contemporary art quilters, modern quilters do not seem to favor this construction technique.

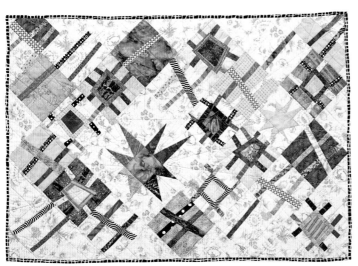

MADE BY CHERYL: All

Fabric at Play

Obviously, fabric plays a central role in quiltmaking. Modern quilting takes fabric and its importance to another level. Many modern quilts can be seen as showcases for fabric, as opposed to the fabric being only one player in the finished quilt. However, the fabric can be subdued to let the quiet nature of modern quilts' simple designs shine.

THE CELEBRITY DESIGNER

The cult status of some fabric designers and their lines of fabric is legendary in the modern quilt world. Fabric designers have their own websites, blogs, Flickr groups, and fan pages. Much of this is about promotion of their lines, but it is also making celebrities out of designers and creating a growing demand for their fabrics.

RETURN TO SOLIDS

Solid fabrics aren't new or particularly modern. It did seem, however, that they'd fallen out of favor with contemporary quilters. Tone-on-tone and hand-dyed fabrics were popular for their almost solid effect. Solids, however, have made a comeback and feature quite prominently in modern quilts. They provide a counterpoint to the very busy fabrics available and serve as an excellent background for showpiece quilting.

SINGLE-FABRIC-LINE QUILTS

Hand in hand with the celebrity designer is the quilt made from a single line of fabric. Quilters are eager to share their love of a fabric line by showcasing the entire line in one quilt, rather than mixing up their favorites with other fabrics.

NOVELTY, LARGE-SCALE, AND GRAPHIC PRINTS

The designs on modern quilting fabrics are nothing short of bold. Sweet and graphic novelty prints of anything from cutlery to fairy-tale themes to animals can be found from many designers. Florals and paisleys on a large scale are also very popular. Graphic prints and geometric designs, also on a larger scale, are growing in popularity. Gone are the calicoes and tiny prints. It is interesting to note, however, that many modern fabrics are inspired by vintage finds.

MADE BY CHERYL: Top left

MADE BY AMANDA JEAN: Top right, bottom left, and bottom right

Color in Action

According to one local shop owner we know, one of the defining features of modern quilts is the use of white. This doesn't just mean the use of white sashing—although we see a lot of that in modern quilts—but the fact that modern fabrics are more white than gray in tone.

CLEAR, BRIGHT COLORS

Regardless of the color of the fabric, modern quilting fabrics are generally more saturated in color and low in tone. That is, if you look for gray or white undertones to the fabric, you will find more white. There is a brightness, or luminosity, to them. The result is a lot of bright quilts.

GRAY IS NOT IGNORED

Despite the dominance of white, gray is also a very popular color in modern quilts. It is a clear, almost cold gray. Again, as in the rest of the modern palette, there is more white than earthy gray in the modern gray.

FORGET THE JEWEL TONES AND EARTH TONES

The richness and earthiness of jewel tones and earthy colorways are rarely seen in modern quilts. If they do creep in, they are used judiciously and do not dominate the color choices.

WHAT COLOR WHEEL?

Pink, yellow, and gray. Red and aqua. Purple, pink, and orange. These may not seem like conventional color choices, but challenging the conventions is part of modern quilting. Modern quilters often push the boundaries of color theory or discard it entirely. Bold choices combined with bold fabrics make for bold quilts.

None of the themes we've discussed here constitute hard-and-fast rules. The most important aspect of quilting is working with what you like, making what you like.

MADE BY AMANDA JEAN: Top left
MADE BY CHERYL: Top right, bottom left, and bottom right

Scrap
Basics

" Leftovers are
a fantastic
thing in the
fabric world."

What Defines a Scrap?

Everyone has a different definition of a scrap—from having used that fabric once before to anything smaller than 2″.

For our purposes, anything ¼ yard (either cut off the bolt or a fat quarter) or larger is considered *stash,* and anything less than ¼ yard is *scrap.*

To further define scraps:

SELVAGES are the tightly woven edges of the fabric. One side is used for registration during printing and usually has dots of color as well as the name of the fabric line and the designer.

SNIPPETS are anything smaller than a 4″ square.

STRINGS are uneven or unmeasured cuts of fabric of any length, in any width up to 2½″.

STRIPS are evenly cut in any width increment—1½″, 2″, 2½″, and so on. Lengths will vary.

SECTIONS are the larger rectangular or square pieces that don't fit in the categories above.

You may have a different term or understanding when describing scraps. We use these terms throughout the book and in the projects, so refer back here if you have questions when reading the instructions for a project.

To be honest, though, it isn't worth getting hung up on whether something is technically a scrap. The quilt police are too busy monitoring missing points and less-than-square blocks to care whether your scrap quilt is 100 percent scrappy.

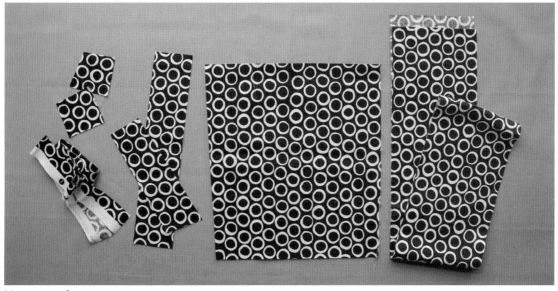

Many types of scraps

From Stash to Scraps

BUYING FABRIC

How you purchase fabric also will increase or decrease your scrap supply. We all buy fabric differently. We know people who only buy for a specific project, and any leftovers automatically become scraps. Some quilters only buy fat quarters. We are the type to purchase yardage. This gives us options both for using our stash in many different ways and for building the scrap pile.

As a default, Cheryl buys ½- to 1-yard pieces of fabric—unless she really, really likes it; then she might buy more, but not usually much more. Most of her stash quilts tend to have a scrappy look to them. That is, they use a lot of different fabrics. That means a stash fabric may remain in the stash for quite a while. Use it a handful of times, and no matter how much you love it, you don't want to see it again!

Amanda usually buys ¼- or ½-yard cuts, and sometimes fat quarters. If she comes across a great sale and she likes the fabric, she will buy 5 yards to use for a backing at a later date. She also loves having a variety of prints to work with and choose from. She tends to buy what she likes; then, when starting a project, she pulls all the fabrics for said project entirely from her stash.

PREWASHING OR NOT

Prewashing is always a big debate among quilters. Neither of us prewashes our fabric—unless we are using batiks or reds. We would both do a light prewash on these as they have a tendency to run. For more on prewashing, see Before You Start Sewing (page 42).

Another reason to prewash both fabric and batting would be if you wanted to minimize the crinkly look in your finished, washed quilt.

CUTTING FABRIC

You can cut fabric to optimize scrap production. All that really means is that when you make the first cut into your stash fabric, you don't do it willy-nilly. If all you need is one strip or a 6½″ × 6½″ charm square, there are good and better ways to cut. Whether you are starting with a fat quarter or a couple of yards of fabric, think about how you use your fabric overall. Is this a good piece for binding? Will you want to use this in big chunks? Is this fabric better chopped up in little pieces or left large?

Our preference is usually to keep the fabric open to long strips. We will always cut it crosswise (selvage to selvage) rather than lengthwise, even if all that is needed is a little piece. This leaves a longer piece of fabric rather than something that gets closer and closer to a fat quarter.

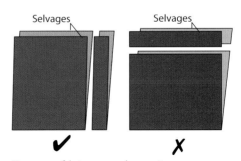

Keep your fabric open to long strips.

Your first cut should always be the selvage edge. Whether you save the selvages or not, cutting them off at the beginning is a lot easier than trimming those pieces later. Even if the print runs all the way to the selvage, that edge is thicker and won't sew as easily. We like to take it off right at the beginning to just get it over with. By cutting it off first you also get a clean, full strip of text and dots. Cut off both selvage edges. Store the ones you might use, and give away or discard the ones you don't want. Frankly, doing it first is also easier because then it is done, and there is one less detail to worry about when cutting the fabric for a project.

Now you are ready to cut your first piece of the fabric. Ignore this step if you are cutting off a small chunk for a little charm or maybe some appliqué. Everyone else, we suggest you follow these instructions:

1. Make sure the fabric is lying straight before you cut strips or you will end up with wavy or V-shaped strips (see Cutting, page 44).

2. Are you fussy cutting the fabric? That is, are you cutting to highlight a certain design or feature on the fabric, trying to match a plaid, or line up stripes? Working from the straightened fabric, make the fussy cuts. If you need multiple fussy cuts, try to use the repeat crosswise through the fabric, not lengthwise. One of the best parts about fussy cutting for a project—aside from the feature pieces, of course—is all those bits in between that are now available to fill up your scrap bin.

Fussy cutting

3. If you are just cutting project pieces, we recommend cutting crosswise. Need a handful of 6½″ × 6½″ charms? Cut a 6½″-wide strip, cut the charms, and put the rest of the strip in the scrap bin. Need only a single 6″ × 6″ block? Cut the strip, cut the block, and then add the leftovers to the scrap bin. Cutting out strips for a Log Cabin or string quilt? Cut that long strip and augment the scrap bin with the leftovers.

DON'T THROW AWAY THOSE SELVAGES!

Selvages were once deemed the unusable parts of fabric. One wouldn't sew with them, but they do contain valuable information about the colors used, manufacturing, and designers or lines. Many beautiful projects, ranging from pincushions to full-sized quilts, now use selvages as a main design element. Check out these sites for inspiration:

- aroundtheblockdesigns.blogspot.com
- flickr.com/groups/quiltsfromselvages
- selvageblog.blogspot.com
- quispamsisquilter.blogspot.com

OPTIMIZING YOUR FABRIC

When cutting from your stash, follow these guidelines:

- Don't cut into the fabric from all sides and end up with an odd chunk of fabric with uneven edges and a weird shape. If you don't like dangly bits messing up your stash, trim them off as you cut for a project.

- Don't leave a bias edge of fabric that you fold and store back with your stash. Cut off any bias bits and add them to the scrap bin because bias edges stretch.

- Don't leave too small of a piece behind. If there is less than a 6″-long strip or less than a fat quarter, you aren't likely to use that fabric in a big way. If it sits in your stash, it will get lost, or you will want to use it, only to discover that you don't have enough left. Retire it to your scrap bin.

Although cutting fabric is almost always going to add to your scrap bin (and we would never complain about that!), cut to keep as much of your stash intact as possible. You want to keep your stash as useful as you can. You never know what you will want that fabric for down the line.

There are a couple of clues.

- Check whether there is a crease in the fabric from being on the bolt (not applicable if prewashed). The selvage edge is parallel to the crease.

- Check the length of the fabric. If it is longer than 44″–45″, the selvage edge is along that longer length, not the short side of the fabric.

- The lengthwise grain is less stretchy than the bias or crosswise grain. With a gentle pull, you can determine the lengthwise grain, and the selvage edge is parallel to this grainline.

USING LEFTOVERS

Which is better, the big turkey dinner or the next day's turkey sandwich? Leftovers are fantastic things in the fabric world as well. This book provides numerous options for using your leftovers, whether you go the direct route of the hot turkey sandwich with the leftover gravy or a fancy sandwich with cheese, apples, and mustard. There is something for everyone.

Several of the quilts in this book rely on a single-color background to tie the scraps together. For example, *Up, Up, and Away* (page 132) uses a single white fabric to unify several hundred tiny triangles. Background fabric, when chosen strategically, does wonders. It unifies many different colors and prints and helps them all get along, as in *Daydreams* (page 66). It also makes your fabric scraps go a long way (that can be a good or a bad thing—you'll have to decide which it is for you). *Checkerboard* (page 128) uses a variety of white and cream prints for the background color, so it uses up odd bits of several different whites while still maintaining the orderly design.

Then there are quilts that use no background fabric at all, only scraps. Some examples are *Scrapper's Delight* (page 82), *The Missing U* (page 102), *Fortune Teller* (page 108), *Splash* (page 72), *Sunday Morning* (page 96), and *High Five* (page 118). These quilts will help you make a serious dent in your scrap bins, since there is no filler.

Eventually, you will whittle your scraps down to little bits. That's when it's a good time to make *The Original Ticker Tape* (page 138) or *Gumdrops* (page 122) quilt.

After making several scrap quilts, you may get your fill of seeing the same scraps over and over again. When we get to that point, we pass the remaining scraps on to a friend. There are only so many times you can use the same fabric before being tired of it. This is the perfect time to swap your scraps with a friend. In fact, that is how many of the quilts in this book came to be—we swapped scraps with others.

Acquiring Scraps

If you are a fairly new quilter, you may not have a scrap stash that feels robust enough to allow you to tackle a scrap quilt. Or, you may not have the range of colors that you want. If you are looking for ways to enhance your scrap stash, here are a few ideas.

- Buy from designers and other quilters; they often sell scrap bags. But keep your eyes open and be prepared to act fast; these always seem to be popular sellers.

- Moda Fabrics sells scrap bags that are color coordinated.

- Search on etsy.com or ebay.com for fabric scraps.

- Find a seamstress who uses designer fabrics for making clothing, particularly for kids. That process produces a lot of scraps that are of little value to a clothing maker but that would make many great quilt pieces. If you don't know a seamstress personally, you could try to locate one through etsy.com or try to find someone through his or her blog.

- Find a friend or fellow quilter who has scraps to share or trade.

- Sometimes bloggers offer up scraps as a giveaway. They benefit everyone involved, even the postal service.

Of course, you can always make more quilts! Definitely some scraps to be found there.

Scrap
Sorting
and
Storage

"...it will
inspire you"

Why Sort?

You may be thinking, "Why sort? What's wrong with a garbage can / laundry basket / plastic bin / suitcase full of bits of fabric in a rainbow of colors? I think it looks pretty." Or maybe the pile is so large that it is too much to face. Or you might not have many scraps, so it doesn't make sense to sort it out.

If you are going to make a lot of scrap quilts—heck, a lot of quilts, period—it's important to have an effective way to sort and store the scraps. They can easily multiply and take over a creative space without much notice. If your scraps are tucked in the back of a closet, the chances are slim that they will ever be used. The old saying "out of sight, out of mind" applies here. If your scraps are all shoved into one big basket, hunting for a specific piece is messy, time consuming, and not for the faint of heart. If your scraps are in some semblance of order, however, it will reduce the time, energy, and frustration involved in making your quilt. And dare we say it? Scrap sorting will be fun!

We want to help you use up as much of your beloved fabric as possible. Personal experience shows that you need a deliberate approach to

sorting in order to maximize your fabric usage. It also helps keep that overwhelmed feeling at bay. Then, make sure that what you do sort is accessible—visible, it will inspire you. Guaranteed.

When it comes down to it, you need to devise a system that truly works for you. It also must reflect the reality of your sewing and storage space.

Ask yourself the following four questions:

1. What do I do with my fabric when cutting for a project?

2. What do I do with the leftovers?

3. Where can I store my scraps?

4. How likely am I to use my scraps?

In the rest of this chapter we will outline the methods we use for sorting and storing our scraps. We're fairly similar in how we approach our scraps, but we have different spaces to work in. That affects how we work with our scraps, but we both want to create exciting, modern quilts. You will see that color is particularly important to our sorting and storage—as are our storage capabilities.

Our Spaces

AMANDA JEAN

I am fortunate to have my very own room for creating. It was a shared space until recently, when my husband moved his office into the basement. My space isn't large—about 9′ × 11′—but I'm thankful to have a dedicated space to create in. Because it is all mine, it also comes with the stipulation that all my creative supplies need to be contained in the one room. Having a dedicated space allows me to leave projects in various states of completion. They sit and wait until I have a chance to get back to them. It's the perfect setup for a busy mom.

Having my own room also affords me adequate space to spread out my many scrap bins. I have a quilted storage box in every color of the rainbow to hold the corresponding scraps. (For directions on how to make your own storage boxes, see page 62.) They make a nice addition, both functionally and aesthetically, to my creative space. The fact that they are handmade is icing on the cake.

One of my very favorite features of the room is my design wall. It's simply a flat flannel sheet tacked onto the wall. It covers nearly the entire wall and it allows me to lay out my quilt blocks as I make them. This is a good place not only to arrange the blocks as I work out the design, but also to store them until they are assembled into a quilt top. It makes for an ever-changing wall of artwork.

Amanda Jean's creative space

CHERYL

My house is small—1,100 square feet. In this house my husband and I raise our little girls, work at our respective businesses (we're both self-employed), cook daily, pick up after each other and the dog, and generally laugh the day away. It is a crazy, colorful, and creative home. This also means that it's crowded and somewhat chaotic.

All of my sewing and writing take place at the dining room table, where we also create with the girls, eat, and run the home and our businesses. There is a lot of packing and moving of things on a daily basis. My fabric is stored in one of the two bedrooms, but I keep current projects in bins that can move between the dining room and the closet.

Once I actually sort my scraps, they go back into the fabric closet, stored in bins beside the rest of my fabrics. There are two storage options in the dining room as well. Large canisters hold the scraps that come from cutting, such as selvages, and a small wire basket holds the current project scraps. I'll admit—it overflows a lot. It does, however, make a great play toy for the girls! In all honesty, it also forces me to sort and store frequently.

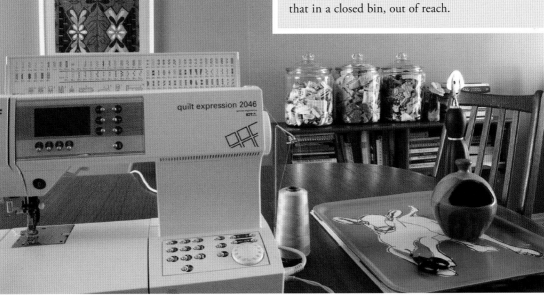

Cheryl's creative hub

Sorting Your Scraps

If you have never sorted your scraps, the initial sort can be daunting, but we encourage you to go for it. We've both tried the "throw it all into one big basket" method, and we can both say from experience that sorting is better. Be prepared; it will take time. After the scraps are sorted and the system is in place, the maintenance of the system is fairly painless. You may find that you need to add or subtract a bin as projects are started and completed. That's perfectly fine. Change and adapt your system as necessary, but to get started, follow these steps.

Unsorted scraps

1. SORT BY COLOR

First and foremost, we strongly recommend sorting scraps by color. It is by far the easiest to begin a quilt with a color concept. Searching for all your scraps in a multicolor bin will be enough to kill any motivation you have to start. The thrill of the hunt only carries you so far. Many of the projects in this book are based on a bold use of color. Having easy access to all your scraps of a single color family will make your creative process run more smoothly. Other reasons that sorting by color makes sense:

- Color itself is inspiring. A pile of red fabrics, for example, next to a pile of orange begs for a sunset- or fire-inspired quilt. The aqua next to the orange screams out for a modern and on-trend design such as *Splash* (page 72).

- It helps you see what colors you use most. This lets you know that it's either time for a change or time to go shopping for other colors.

- If your storage is visible, it is easy to pick out scraps when needed, instead of digging through your stash for one small piece of blue.

- For obsessive types (like us), sorting by color is calming and encourages creativity.

- For free spirits, it doesn't slow down the creative process—you can find what you need faster.

- Modern quilt design is strongly rooted in bold and creative uses of color. An organized scrap collection contributes to that creative aesthetic in your own studio.

Now that we have you convinced to sort by color, you need to get started on the sort. Most likely you will be in one of two categories: You have your scraps in a giant bin, but they aren't sorted, or you've never sorted and everything is considered stash. Even if you've been sorting all along, there is still good organizational stuff here for you, so keep reading.

If you already have a laundry basket full of scraps, the first step is to dump all your scraps on a table, the floor, or a bed—whatever is the easiest spot for you.

If your scraps are hiding among the stash, then we suggest that you go through your stash color by color, one piece at a time. Trim off errant ends, odd cuts, and dangly bits. Return the pieces that are bigger than a fat quarter to your stash. And yes, take the time to fold each piece. Put the rest in the scrap pile. Even if you already have your scraps stored separately from your stash, it is still a great idea to go through your stash to clean out any potential scraps.

Now, put your scraps in piles by color. Don't worry about value, tint, or shade. Just go by color. If a piece is multicolored, either start a unique pile for multicolored fabrics or go with the dominant or background color of the fabric.

If you are just beginning on your quiltmaking journey and you don't have a robust scrap stash yet, you may want to start by sorting your scraps into three simple categories: warms, cools, and neutrals.

Remove snippets and strings of fabric, regardless of color, and place each in its own pile. More on these shortly.

2. DETERMINE YOUR STORAGE REQUIREMENTS

Decide what storage system makes the most sense based on your needs and space. Is it worth having a bin for each color? What space do you have to store the scraps? How many bins, containers, or drawers do you need? Go shopping, at home or at the store. For more storage options, see page 38.

3. PUT AWAY THE FABRIC

Put away the fabric as soon as you can after finishing the sort. You may not have a choice if it is on the dining room table. Minimize the chance for grabby hands and pets to mess up all your hard work.

Color sorting will take you through the rainbow: You'll likely need bins for red, orange, yellow, green, blue, purple, and pink—with another bin for whites, grays, browns, and blacks. Add a bin for multicolored fabrics. This bin is a sanity saver. Many fabrics are multicolored, such as stripes, florals, and novelty prints, making them hard to sort. This bin holds them all.

With a basic color sort out of the way, you can proceed to the next level of sorting. Remember all those little bits we told you to keep aside? Let's tackle those now.

THOSE OH-SO-SPECIAL FABRICS

With the proliferation of designer fabrics and even celebrity designers, many quilters want to keep collections of fabrics together, right down to the scraps. Although this isn't the way either of us works, we do see it all the time among friends. If this is you, make little scrap bins so you can keep your designer fabric scraps with each designer fabric collection. Then you can do an all-collection scrap version of one of the great quilts in this book.

Snippets, Strings, Selvages, and More

Inevitably, any sewing project will result in little snippets and strings of fabric. Small, odd-sized, or seemingly unusable bits of fabric have a life beyond helping squirrels build their nests.

We find it much easier to keep the little bits of scraps sorted separately from the rest of the lot. For the designs in this book, we've used pieces as small as 1″. And some strings and strips can be just as thin. Those small bits will easily get lost or tangled in a bin full of larger pieces. That's why we recommend storing them separately. They will be easier to find and more likely to be used.

While we both sort by color and separate our little bits of fabric scraps, we do differ in exactly what we save and how we differentiate the pieces. What is important is coming up with a sorting and saving system that works for you and your space. Here are some categories for these minisorts that may be helpful and inspiring for you.

2½″ × 2½″ SQUARES: The most basic of quilt shapes, squares this size are used for *Checkerboard* (page 128).

BINDING TRIANGLES: Left over from joining binding strips on the diagonal, triangles this size are used in *Up, Up, and Away* (page 132).

SELVAGES: Loads of quilters collect selvages to use on some very creative projects. (We've got some inspiration links for you on page 23.)

SMALL SNIPPETS: Odd cuts and small bits coming in around 1″–2″ are great for *The Original Ticker Tape* (page 138). Doll-sized ticker tape quilts are a good approach for using them up without having a huge, daunting project hanging over your head.

SNIPPETS: Anything less than 4″ is great to keep separate from your colored sort because these pieces are easily grabbed to fill in space on projects such as *Gumdrops* (page 122) and *Grass* (page 76), and for the appliqué in *Leaves and Vine* (page 112). You also can trim these pieces as necessary to make 2½″ × 2½″ squares, triangles, or small snippets.

STRINGS: Uneven cuts of various lengths are perfect for *Grass* (page 76) and *Scrapper's Delight* (page 82).

2½″ STRIPS: Strips can be used to make coins or squares, or you can piece them all together and make a scrappy binding, as in *Gumdrops* (page 122).

SKINNY STRIPS: Measuring ½″–1″ wide, these strips may seem small for piecing, but they can indeed be used.

Only you will know the best way to sort and store these little bits. It goes back to the four questions we asked at the beginning of the chapter: *What do I do with my fabric when cutting for a project? What do I do with the leftovers? Where can I store my scraps? How likely am I to use my scraps?* The projects in this book will get you using all your favorite fabric, from your stash to the smallest bits.

KNIT A FABRIC MAT

If you are very serious about using up every last bit of fabric, as Amanda Jean has a tendency to do, even those skinny strips and trimmed selvages can be used. The best way is in a simple knitting project, as there is little to no seam allowance left on the fabric. Join the strings by knotting the ends together to make a long string of fabric. Use two strands of string/strips held together throughout to knit. You can easily make a thick rug, suitable for any room of the house—it even makes a perfect bath mat. Use size 17 needles. Cast on 34 stitches, knit in garter stitch to the desired length, and then bind off all the stitches.

Mat knit from fabric scraps

EVOLUTION OF ORGANIZATION

There was a time when Cheryl didn't keep scraps. Small snippets went into a plastic bag to be donated to someone else. Everything else went back into her stash. With more and more quilts came more and more scraps. Those quilts also became scrappier. That is, they used small bits of a lot of different fabrics. Faced with bags of bits of fabric, she knew it was time to do something.

Without a second thought, she started sorting her piles by color. It was the only way she thought to do it, and she still stands by that. But in every bag of color went pieces of every size. That was fine at first, but it wasn't very efficient. It didn't work when she was working on something multicolored, or when she needed a more specific size.

Amanda Jean suggested that she separate out the snippets. It was great advice and made production a lot faster and easier. Then, on one of her last sorts, she started a pile for strings without even thinking about it. It really is an instinctual way to sort when you sit down to the task.

Just through the process of creating and writing this book, Cheryl's scrap sorting and storage method evolved. Perhaps it was all the late nights getting the book together and the full immersion in the text. Or maybe it was simply facing the reality of the scraps and the types of quilts she produces.

Scrap sorting and storage is not a one-time-only task. Your system will change as the quilts you make change, as your space changes, and as your time and inclination change. Cheryl's experience proves that. But a solid system with some groundwork makes staying organized painless and even inspiring.

Going Forward

There is a difference between getting organized and staying organized. After you've tackled the great color sort, you need to store those scraps in such a way that they stay sorted, are accessible, and fit within your space. The next section outlines a number of options.

Now it is time to implement a scrap management system. Our biggest recommendation is to *keep a small bin or basket next to your cutting table.* Place scraps in this bin or basket as they emerge from a project. At the end of the project or as soon as the basket is full, place those scraps in their designated color bins. The Quilted Storage Box (page 62) is a perfect solution.

Quilted Storage Box

Storage Ideas

Whether you have a dedicated sewing studio or are sharing a space with kids, dogs, and a husband, there are many storage options for your scraps. What is most important is putting your scraps where they are easily accessible and hopefully visible.

We also like storage methods that allow us to keep the fabric neat. When you throw your scraps in a bin or a bag it works well for organization, but when it comes to using those fabrics you add more sorting and lots of ironing as extra steps to your sewing.

Drawers or baskets that allow you to store scraps flat go a long way toward creating scrap enjoyment. If you don't have the space or resources for something like that, fold or roll your fabrics instead of stuffing them all together willy-nilly.

Below are a few of our favorite storage ideas. They range from inexpensive items that you can pick up at any big box or craft store to dedicated pieces of furniture. Enjoy our tour of options, plus a small project to help you get started on scrap storage.

- Big glass jars that you might normally use to store flour and sugar
- Vintage canisters and lunch boxes
- Hanging toy cubbies
- Tool chests—those big red or charcoal chests usually reserved for screwdrivers
- Buckets spray painted the color of the scraps stored inside
- Plain canvas totes or bins, decorated with fabric paint or with a swatch of fabric
- Plastic containers
- See-through shoeboxes from a discount store
- Regular shoeboxes

- Shoe hangers—the kind that hang in your closet with cubbies for shoes
- Transparent plastic food containers, thoroughly washed (clamshell containers or containers that have removable lids, such as those used for strawberries or leaf lettuce, for example)
- Gift bags—plain or decorated
- Small stacked drawer organizers
- Baskets
- Old wooden bowls
- A dresser or drawers in a dresser with sock sorters inserted
- Brown paper bags

Many, many scrap storage options

Scrap Sorting and Storage   39

Many, many more scrap storage options

Quilt Construction Basics

"Modern would not be modern without knowing the tradition behind it."

It's hard to acquire a mess of scraps without knowing a few quiltmaking basics. We realize that we all have our own ways of tackling a project and the many steps to completion. With more than 250 quilts between us, you can be sure we've learned a thing or two since those beginner classes. We're sharing those things with you here.

This chapter also contains our most basic construction technique for many of the quilts in this book—sewing a slab of fabric. This essentially means you are creating fabric from your scraps. Use these slabs to make blocks, backgrounds, and anything else you need to make scrap quilts. It is an improvisational technique, so be prepared to break free from your templates and precision cutting.

Because this is a modern quilt book, you may think that the basics of quilting no longer apply. We wholeheartedly disagree. Wonky does not equal sloppy. It always pays to cut, piece, and press carefully and accurately. Modern would not be modern without knowing the tradition behind it.

Before You Start Sewing

FABRIC

We're talking about scrap quilts so it may seem contradictory to say that you should use only cotton fabrics in your quilts, so we won't say it. We do, however, have a preference for quilting cottons when we work. That being said, linens, linen blends, knits, wools, home décor–weight fabrics, and even silks can all be used successfully in quilts. To save yourself a lot of headaches, we generally recommend not mixing different types of fabrics in one quilt. You should also not expect to use the same thread, needles, and sewing tension when working with different fabrics.

There are times when you do want to combine different types of fabric in your scrap quilts. Again, we see nothing wrong with that. But be prepared for different materials to behave differently, and take your time when working.

When it comes to quilting cottons, we usually don't prewash our fabrics. The exceptions: we always prewash batiks and usually prewash reds. Generally, if you are concerned that a color will run, either prewash it or at least test it to see if it runs. To test it, wet a corner of the fabric in a white or light-colored sink. If the water is anything but clear, prewash and dry. Test again. Repeat until the color doesn't run. Consider using a color-setting product such as Retayne.

If we aren't concerned with color running, we generally don't bother with prewashing. We realize that this is entirely a personal matter for quilters. There are no hard-and-fast rules. Stick with what you are most comfortable doing.

SIZE

Although there are times when we don't know where we'll end up when we start a project, usually the first thing we know is how big we want it to be—a precious baby quilt, something for the couch, or a new bed quilt. All our projects can be sized up or down. Here are some easy ways to tackle changing the size of a quilt design.

- Add or subtract blocks or rows. You can usually do this without affecting the design.

- Make the blocks themselves bigger or smaller. This is the better option when adding or subtracting blocks will change the overall design.

- Add a creative border. Sure, you can throw a large-print border around your blocks and call it a day, but a pieced border will be much more interesting.

TOOLS

Having a basic set of tools is important for any quilter, the modern one included. We recommend the following basic tool kit:

Working sewing machine

Neutral thread in gray and cream for piecing

Range of sewing machine needles in various sizes for both piecing and quilting (Start with a 75/11 or 70/10 universal needle for piecing. Your quilting needle size will depend on the thread and the quilt itself.)

Hand sewing needles

Rotary cutter—45mm or 60mm size with a new blade

Self-healing cutting mat, minimum of 16″ × 24″

Steam iron and ironing board with washable cover

Clear acrylic rotary cutting rulers—at least one 16″ long and one square, preferably 12½″ × 12½″

Scissors reserved for cutting fabric

Straight pins at least 1½″ long and appliqué pins

Pincushion

Pencil or marking pencil

Duct tape or masking tape

Curved safety pins

Freezer paper

You will add to, and probably subtract from, this list; the tools and notions you choose to maintain will be personal. It will depend on the quilts you like to make, your addiction to notions, and any tidbits you've found to make your sewing more enjoyable.

CUTTING

Before you can start sewing, you need to cut the fabric. When it comes off the bolt it isn't ready to be cut. Here are the steps for successfully cutting new fabric.

1. Press the fabric well to eliminate as many folds and wrinkles as possible. If you prewash your fabric, press it well when you take it from the dryer *and* just before cutting (to eliminate any folds and creases from storage).

2. Whether you are saving selvages or not, cut them off after pressing.

3. Create a straight edge from which to make all your cuts. After pressing, line up the selvage edges as close to even as possible. Hold the selvage edges in your fingers, keeping all the fabric up off the cutting table. Does the fabric hang straight down with no waves in the fabric? Yes? Then proceed to the next step. No? Then adjust the selvages in your fingers, making one side higher or lower, until the wobbliness disappears. Now proceed.

4. Carefully place the fabric on a cutting mat. Line up a guideline of the ruler on the fold of the fabric. The ruler should be perpendicular to the fabric—exactly 90°. If the ruler isn't exactly square on the fabric, the strip will have a V shape near the fold. The purpose of the first cut is to give the fabric a nice clean edge—a starting point, if you will. Make the remaining cuts as necessary. If you are making a number of cuts, periodically repeat the process of squaring up the fabric. Whenever possible, use the ruler rather than the cutting mat to measure the fabric. Cutting mats can distort with repeated use.

Fabric is uneven.

Fabric is flat and ready to cut.

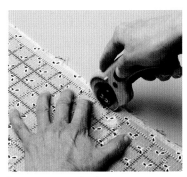

Lining up to make first cut

Photos by C&T Publishing

The Hum of the Machine

With the fabric selected and cut, it is time to sit down and sew. Knowing a few tips to make the sewing process run smoothly will make the entire quiltmaking endeavor easier. The basic concepts may seem obvious, but you'd be quite surprised by how many quilters gloss over them. Then they wonder why they are having so much trouble finishing their quilts!

PIECING

A ¼″ seam allowance is a good skill to perfect. Although many of the quilts in this book don't rely on precision piecing—no fussy star points here—it is necessary to maintain neat working habits. Skimping on the ¼″ seam will only cause problems such as popped seams or blocks that won't lie flat. Crooked seams will manifest themselves as bubbles or tucks in the quilt.

Here are ways to achieve a more accurate ¼″ seam allowance:

* Use a ¼″ presser foot with a guide. This is sometimes called a compensating presser foot. This is a ¼″ foot, but the feature that makes it unique is that it also has a guide to the right. The fabric feeds through as it would with a normal presser foot, while the guide on the foot helps you maintain a consistent seam allowance. This foot attachment is machine specific, so read your sewing machine manual or check with the sewing machine dealer to see what your options are.

* Use tape. Adding a piece of tape on the machine as a guide is an inexpensive and simple fix. Place the needle in the down position. Use a ruler to measure ¼″ to the right of the needle and then adhere the tape. Guide the fabric along the tape line when piecing. Using foam tape (as long as there is no residue of glue on the raised sides) would work as well.

* Magnetic seam guides are available, which could work on any machine with a metal throat plate. They are not recommended for computerized machines, so check with the dealer before using one on your machine.

* Use the fast2sew Ultimate Seam Guide. It's a plastic template for machines that provides a clear ¼″ seamline.

Then there's always practice, for which there is no substitute.

Also on the topic of piecing, pick a neutral-color thread. If you are using light fabrics, choose a white or cream thread. For all other colors or a light/dark combo, we recommend using gray thread.

PRESSING

Pressing seam by seam is a necessary part of quiltmaking. It promotes neatness and accuracy. Pressing is fairly straightforward, but we want to share a few tips to help you fine-tune your ironing experience.

First of all, when you press, it is important not to pull or distort the fabric. It is best to place the quilt block on the ironing board and first set the seam by pressing on it directly, very briefly. Then, letting the iron do the work, gently press the seam to one side. It has been said that you should be able to press your fabric with one hand behind your back. While neither of us does this all the time, it is a good exercise to practice, especially if you tend to pull, stretch, or distort your fabric when you are working.

We realize that many quilters prefer to press their seams open. Although we aren't fans of that practice because we find it gives us more popped seams, press the way you are most comfortable.

Within a single scrap quilt, potentially hundreds of different fabrics will be used. The weight and feel of the fabrics vary quite a bit, even under the umbrella of quilting cottons. With all the different fabrics, plus the plethora of seams in a block, sometimes it's hard to get things to lie flat. Use these tools and techniques to help—but also consider the drawbacks.

Take Care of Your Iron

Follow the instructions that come with the iron and regularly clean both the soleplate and the inside water tank.

STEAM IRON:

The pros: No spray bottles are necessary—just the push of a button and the steam appears.

The cons: The iron can collect dust, or even bits of rust inside. When the steam feature is used, those particles can transfer to the fabric and can get the fabric dirty or ruin the quilt block completely.

SPRAY BOTTLE WITH ONLY WATER INSIDE:

The pros: Spray bottles are inexpensive and can be found at many discount stores or even dollar stores. Water is readily available, and it leaves no residue. Gently spritz the block with a fine mist of water, and press with a hot iron on the cotton setting.

The cons: If the spray setting isn't adjusted correctly, the quilt block can get too wet, which can lead to scorched fabric.

SPRAY STARCH:

Spray starch can be purchased, or you can make it in your own kitchen for a couple of cents per bottle.

The pros: Spray starch will keep the block flat even after a lot of handling.

The cons: Sometimes starch can flake. If you make your own starch, and the cornstarch-to-water ratio (page 47) is off-balance or the starch isn't shaken well, the starch can show up on some fabrics, especially darks. This is only a temporary problem, as the starch will come out after washing.

TRIMMING

Always, always, always square up your blocks and trim errant corners before you sew the blocks into a quilt. Even when working improvisationally, there comes a point when you should be taking the ruler and rotary cutter to the block to square it up. Doing it block by block helps keep your quilt square and lightens the load down the line.

Likewise, trim overhangs and seam allowances as you go. This will help your block lie flat and make quilting easier.

HOMEMADE SPRAY STARCH

12–16 oz. water

1½ teaspoons cornstarch

1. Mix the above ingredients well in a glass measuring cup until no lumps remain, and pour into a spray bottle.

2. Add 2–3 drops of lavender essential oil and shake well.

The starch will separate, so shake before each use. Keep in the refrigerator (or discard) when not in use for long periods of time.

SEWING A SLAB OF FABRIC

Many of the designs in *Sunday Morning Quilts* rely on the slab concept: sewing scraps together to make a piece of fabric. You can make the slab as large or small as you want. After you get used to the technique, it can be quite addictive!

1. Start with a single color of scraps to work with. Sort the scraps into light, medium, and dark piles, as well as a multicolored pile (that includes colors other than the one you are working with). Then sort each pile by value. Make as many piles as you need to feel comfortable with the color and values. (Figure A)

Choose a few piles to work with. There should be some variety in the colors and values, but not a wide range. This selection process will take some getting used to but will become more natural over time and with practice. Press the pieces you've selected to work with.

2. Start by working with 2 of the smaller-sized scraps that are roughly the same size. With right sides together, sew them together. Press and trim any overhanging ends.

3. Find another scrap that works next to the first 2 fabrics. With right sides together, sew; then press and trim the ends. (Figure B)

Start Small

We encourage you to start with the smaller pieces and ones that are roughly the same size because it will use up scraps rather than making more in the process. Plus, the larger pieces can be used for longer strips as the slab grows in size.

Sort scraps by value.

Start with 2 smaller-sized scraps and add on.

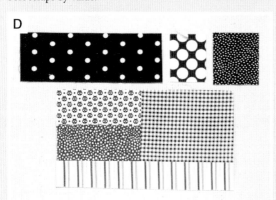

Piece 2 or more scraps together to make a longer strip.

Use offset seams.

Sewing a Slab of Fabric

4. Repeat, adding to any side at any time. Offset the seams as you add pieces to the slab. This adds interest and makes it easier, as there are no seams to match. It's all about making it work! If you need a longer piece of fabric, sew 2 together end to end. If you need a shorter piece, trim it to length. If, after piecing a strip, it comes up short compared to the slab, don't be afraid to trim the slab to fit your strip. (Figures C–F)

5. Continue to sew and press until you've created a slab a bit larger than the desired size. Give the slab a good press and trim it down to the needed size. Add a quick zigzag or straight stitch ⅛″ in from the outside edge all around the block to prevent the seams from splitting.

This will save much frustration later when assembling the final pieces into a quilt top. (Figure G)

Every single slab you make will be unique. Over time you will likely develop a personal rhythm and style. Play around with this technique and have fun with it!

Sewing a Slab of Fabric

It's Okay to Change Your Mind

Don't worry if you decide you want to add on after you've sewn the stay stitch around the outside edge. That stitch is contained in the seam allowance, so it is easy to make changes or additions to the slab at any point.

Don't Trim Yet

Don't worry about trimming or squaring up your scraps at this point. An off-kilter look adds interest to the finished slab. As a bonus, you are really using all your fabric scraps.

Keep adding to slab.

Keep adding on until desired size is reached.

Finished slab with stay stitching around edges

Turning the Pieced Top into a Quilt

So many of us stop once we have a finished quilt top. But that isn't the only exciting part of quiltmaking. Seeing it come together as a final product is thrilling. Besides, you can't use it until it becomes a quilt.

The following tips are for quilting a project on your own. If you really want to get it done, don't hesitate to send it to a pro for quilting—whatever it takes to get you snuggling sooner.

BACKING

By far the easiest way to make a quilt back is to buy enough of one fabric to seam together the backing.

Piecing the Backing

It might be easier to piece a back from yardage by simply sewing two long pieces of fabric together, but this isn't the best for your quilt. We tend to fold quilts down the middle, and if you have a seam in your quilt back down the middle, it encourages more wear in the quilt. Try to split the fabric in three to piece the back. Use one full width of yardage in the middle, and then cut another piece in two. Sew these to either side of the full width of fabric. Two seams are better than one.

Buying a sheet for the back is also possible, but it is not recommended. The thread count of sheets is much higher than that of quilting cottons and linens. It can present a whole host of challenges when quilting. It's doable, but is usually not the best or easiest option.

All the patterns in this book provide you with the yardage needed to make a backing. You might, however, want to consider making a pieced back. Do you have leftover blocks from making the front? Can't decide on a favorite fabric? Don't have enough of any one fabric for a complete back? Break free from the large print or solid for the back and get creative. Think of the back of your quilt as another design opportunity. Piece the back with multiple fabrics, or break up the expanse with blocks, strips, or some improvised piecing.

Our only note of caution is that when you have a lot of seams on the front, go for a simple back without too many seams. We also recommend considering how you will quilt the top before you make a final decision on the back. Numerous seams on the back can cause your machine to trip up and skip stitches when you quilt—so save yourself from headaches by planning ahead.

Pieced backings

QUILT SANDWICH

The quilt sandwich consists of three layers: the backing, the batting, and the quilt top. The process of holding the layers of the quilt sandwich together is called basting. There's no doubt about it—this step is tedious. However, taking the time to do it properly results in easier quilting and, ultimately, a beautifully finished product.

Basting

There are a few options for basting: thread basting with large stitches, spray basting, basting guns (which use little plastic tabs to hold the layers together), or pin basting. We both prefer to pin baste our quilts. It is straightforward and there are no messy fumes to worry about or long threads to contend with.

Items you will need:

- Curved safety pins
- Duct tape (painter's tape or masking tape could be used in a pinch)
- Clip tool for closing the pins or a teaspoon
- Flat surface larger than the quilt (floor or tables)

Note: Do not try this on carpet!

1. Piece or cut the batting so it is 4″ larger on each side than the quilt top. The backing should be approximately the same size as the batting. Press the top well.

2. Tape the backing, right side down, to the floor. Start in the middle and work your way out to the corners. Work on all sides at the same time.

When taping, pull the fabric taut, but don't stretch it. When it is taped down, there should be a piece of tape every 12″–18″ around the perimeter of the quilt.

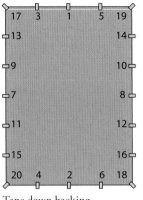

Tape down backing.

3. Place the batting on the quilt back. Smooth out any wrinkles or bumps. Pick off any threads or lint.

4. Press the quilt top and place it on top of the batting. Smooth out the quilt top, working out from the center to the sides and corners.

5. Now it's time to pin. If you are going to quilt near the seamlines, pin in the center of the blocks. If you are going to quilt in the center of the blocks, pin on or near the seamlines. If an allover meandering pattern is going to be used, place the pins randomly throughout. Place pins every 4″, or about a hand width apart. When in doubt, place more pins rather than less. The pins help prevent shifting of the layers until the piece is quilted. The pins will be removed one at a time during the quilting process.

Save Your Knees and Back

Seek out tables and a space large enough to accommodate your quilt. Boardroom tables and banquet tables are perfect for basting. Consider hitting the office early in the morning to take advantage of the tables. Or see if you can borrow a space at a church or a community hall. Many quilt stores also will let you use their space to baste, provided no classes are in session.

QUILTING

Quilting can be hand quilting, free-motion quilting, or walking-foot quilting.

Hand quilting isn't something that either Cheryl or Amanda Jean does on a regular basis. It is, however, a nice touch to add to appliqué or a few simple blocks. We did just that on *Leaves and Vine* (page 112).

Free-motion quilting is our favorite technique. There are many possibilities, and to give you some ideas we've included notes about quilting for each quilt project in this book.

A great in-depth resource is *A Guide to Free-Motion Quilting* by Diane Gaudynski. Although her approach to quilting is much more traditional than we prefer, it is a good technical reference. A good source of ideas for quilting designs is *Modern Quilting Designs* by Bethany Pease (from C&T Publishing).

Walking-foot quilting is more versatile than most people realize. There is more to it than stitching in-the-ditch and echoing seamlines. For instance, use a walking foot to make several wavy lines in a quilt. Use those wavy lines to make a free-form grid as in *Splash* (page 72). Or overlap wavy lines and use them only vertically (think of seaweed) or only horizontally (think of gentle ocean waves). Concentric-square quilting is a good option for highlighting large square sections, as in *The Missing U* (page 102) or the white squares in *Fortune Teller* (page 108). Try using several parallel (or nearly parallel) lines about ¼″–½″ apart, as in the orange section of *Splash* (page 72).

CLEANING UP

Do you remember that we suggested making the batting and backing a few inches larger than the quilt top? That extra fabric is great when quilting and for ensuring that nothing gets shorted, but once you've finished quilting, it needs to go.

Using the longest ruler you have, trim off the excess batting and backing by lining up your ruler with the quilt top edge on the ¼″ mark. That is, the quilt top edge is at ¼″ and the ruler edge is ¼″ out from the quilt edge. Trim around the quilt. Make sure you get right angles at the corners.

The edge of the quilt top should always be on the ¼″ mark. Pull the entire sandwich from the edge, as necessary, to make this happen. If required, plan to block (page 58) the quilt after the first wash.

Trim excess backing and batting ¼″ beyond quilt top.

BINDING BASICS

In this book, the patterns include the binding requirements, but if you want to change the size of any quilt, the following explains how to calculate the amount of fabric and the number of binding strips that are needed.

Number of binding strips

1. Add together the measurements of the 4 sides of the quilt top. For instance, if the quilt is 60″ × 72″, add 60 + 60 + 72 + 72 for a total of 264.

2. The usable width of fabric is 40″ (just to be on the safe side), so divide the total measured lengths (calculated in Step 1) by the usable width of fabric: 264″ ÷ 40″ = 6.6, which rounds up to 7. The number of binding strips needed for a 60″ × 72″ quilt is 7.

Yardage required for binding

Binding strips are usually cut either 2¼″ or 2½″ wide. To determine the yardage required, multiply the number of strips needed by 3″, just to ensure that you have enough fabric. For example, 7 strips × 3″ = 21″, or ⅝ yard.

Making the binding

1. Cut the required number of strips. Trim off any selvages and make sure the ends are cut at a 90° angle.

2. Fold the end of a strip at a 45° angle and press. Pin to another strip, lining up the fold lines.

3. Sew on the fold lines and trim off the excess triangles, leaving a ¼″ seam allowance. Save these binding triangles for *Up, Up, and Away* (page 132). Press the seams to the side. Fold the binding strip in half lengthwise and press. Repeat for all the strips.

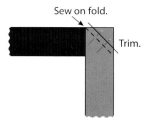

Joining binding strips

At this point we offer two different ways to attach the binding to the quilt and miter the corners.

Method 1

1. Place the binding strip around the perimeter of the quilt. This step will show you where the seams will land, so you can avoid having any seams on the corners, as the bulk will not lie flat or miter well.

2. Starting about a third of the way down a side, place a pin at the beginning of the binding strip. Place another pin 10″ down from the first pin. The 10″ tail will be used for joining the starting and ending points. Sew from the second pin to ¼″ away from the first corner of the quilt. Backstitch a few stitches and remove the quilt from the sewing machine.

3. Fold the binding up, away from the quilt. (Figure A)

4. Pull the binding strip down over itself and align the fold with the edge of the quilt. Pin. (Figure B)

5. Start stitching ¼″ from the top and sew along the side of the quilt to ¼″ from the next corner. Repeat Steps 3 and 4. When all 4 corners are finished, sew until you are about 10″ from the first pin. Backstitch a few stitches.

6. Take the quilt out of the machine. If the binding is 2½″ wide, measure out a 2½″ overlap of fabric. Trim off the excess fabric. (Figure C)

7. Open up the binding strips. With the tail on the left, iron or finger-press a seam on the diagonal.

8. Pin the right-hand tail to the left-hand tail, right sides together, placing the strips perpendicular to each other.

9. Sew on the fold line, trim the excess triangles, and press the seam to one side. (Figure D)

10. Fold the binding in half lengthwise again and align the binding strip to the edge of the quilt.

11. Pin at 6″ intervals and sew the binding, overlapping the stitching at the starting and ending points by ½″. Sew down the binding on the back with your preferred method.

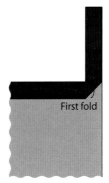

A. Stop stitching ¼″ from corner, remove quilt from machine, and fold binding up.

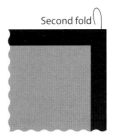

B. Fold binding down.

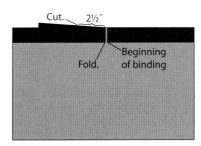

C. Overlap ends and trim.

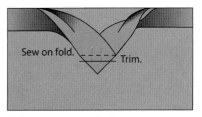

D. Sew on crease and trim.

Method 2

1. Cut binding strips to the appropriate length for each side plus 2″ of overhang at each corner. (Figure A)

2. Pin the binding, one side only, starting ¼″ from the edge of the quilt top. Start sewing the binding at the first pin (leaving a tab of fabric, which we'll deal with shortly). Sew to ¼″ from the bottom corner of the quilt top. Backstitch at the beginning and end. (Figure B)

3. To attach the second binding strip, fold the first strip back at a 45° angle at the end of the stitching. Finger-press. (Figure C)

4. Pin the second strip as you did the first and start sewing ¼″ from the edge. This should be exactly where you finished sewing the previous strip, which should be folded out of the way. Sew down the second strip to ¼″ from the edge of the quilt top. Repeat on the remaining sides. (Figure D)

5. With this technique, each corner is mitered individually. Confirm that your stitches attaching the binding meet but do not overlap. Fix if necessary. (Figure E)

6. Place the quilt on a flat surface. Facing a corner, arrange the flaps so that the folded edges line up to the left. (The horizontal flap will be folded up at a 45° angle and lie beneath the vertical flap, as when you stitched the binding on.) Measure the distance between the folded edge of the binding and the start of the seam for the horizontal binding. It should be 1″ for a 2½″ binding strip. Draw a light horizontal line with a pencil (don't worry—this will be the inside of the binding). Mark the halfway point of this line. (Figure F)

7. From that midpoint, mark a new point above it that is exactly as far from the midpoint as the midpoint is from the binding's folded edge and the binding's seamline (in this case, ½″). (Figure G)

8. Draw a line from the folded edge of the first line up to the second point you marked and down to the start of the stitching. This creates the short legs of a right-angle triangle; these short legs are the seamline. (Figure H)

9. Pin the binding strips together (avoid pinning to the quilt). Fold the corner of the quilt diagonally and pull the binding strips away from the edge, maintaining their alignment. (Figure I)

10. Start stitching on the line at the folded edge. Sew slowly until you get to the peak of the triangle. Stop with the needle down. Pivot and continue sewing until you reach the stitch line, being careful not to sew the binding to the quilt as you reach the end of the line. Repeat on the remaining corners. (Figure J)

11. Trim the excess fabric in the corners. Use small, pointy scissors or a small stick to turn the corners right side out sharply. Sew down the binding on the back with your preferred method. (Figure K)

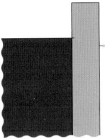

A. Cut binding strips with 2″ overhang.

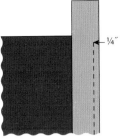

B. Start sewing ¼″ from edge of quilt top.

C. Fold previous strip at 45° angle and place next binding strip for sewing.

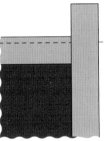

D. Pin next strip and start sewing ¼″ from edge of quilt top.

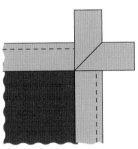

E. Make sure stitches meet but do not overlap.

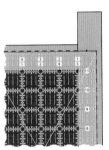

F. Align binding flaps, make horizontal line, and mark midpoint.

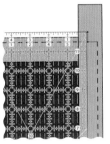

G. Mark new point above midpoint.

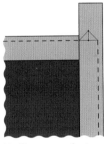

H. Connect endpoints of horizontal line to new point.

I. Fold quilt diagonally and pull binding away from edge.

J. Stitch along line from folded edge to apex; pivot; stitch down to seamline.

K. Turn corners sharply; fold over edge to back and stitch in place.

Finishing Touches

After binding the quilt, trim off any stray or excess thread tails from the front and back.

Add a label, if desired.

WASHING

Washing and drying a quilt is a nice way to break it in and finish it completely. This step will wash away any dirt or oils from all the handling during the construction process. It will remove any excess starch from the assembly process. It also takes the sizing out of the fabrics, which is especially important if you don't prewash your fabrics.

Machine wash in cold water with regular detergent and a color catcher. Tumble dry on medium or low. Remove immediately from the dryer.

BLOCKING

If your quilt was wavy when you trimmed it, consider blocking it.

1. After washing, dry the quilt for just a few minutes to take out any heavy moisture.

2. Place the damp quilt on a flat surface (such as the floor or the lawn) with a clean sheet underneath.

3. Measure through the middle of the quilt vertically and horizontally. Note the measurements and mark the center.

4. Take the vertical measurements of the quilt at the edges and the horizontal measurements of the quilt at the edges. Compare these to those measurements taken through the center. They should match.

5. Measure from the center of the quilt to the corners; these measurements should match.

6. Chances are, at least some of your measurements will not match. Gently pull the edges of the quilt until they do match.

7. As a final check, the diagonal corner-to-opposite-corner measurements should match.

8. Leave flat until dry.

9. Snuggle with the quilt immediately upon finishing.

The Projects

Now that you've sorted and stored all those lovely bits of fabric, let's make quilts. Remember, there are no snuggles if you don't sew.

The projects are organized so that you can take advantage of your scraps from the largest pieces to the smallest. Pick the projects you like, or work through the designs in a systematic approach. Do that and you might end up with no scraps at all! What a perfect excuse to buy new fabric.

"There are no snuggles if you don't sew.

Some of the projects use nothing but scraps, which should put a serious dent in your scrap collection. Other projects feature a white or simple background to showcase your fabric and make the design pop. The variety, we hope, will give you a lot of inspiration. We encourage you to take the design concepts and make the quilts your own. There is no way to recreate these exact quilts because your scraps will be different from ours. Your scraps are yours and your quilts are all you.

Quilted Storage Box

Made by Amanda Jean Nyberg

finished size: 7½″ wide × 5½″ high × 7½″ deep

Use your scraps to make storage boxes for your scraps! These boxes can be made from materials that you probably have on hand already. Make one in every color of the rainbow, and there will never be a doubt about which color of scraps you are reaching for. Or, make them multicolored and label them.

MATERIALS

Makes 1.

- Fabric scraps for box's outside

- Fabric for lining: ¼ yard (fat quarter okay)

- Medium-weight iron-on interfacing, 20″ wide: ⅔ yard

- Batting: 1 square 8½″ × 8½″ and 1 rectangle 17″ × 13″

- Cardboard cereal boxes or other sturdy cardboard (to give box shape and stability—avoid corrugated cardboard, which doesn't bend easily)

- Clear vinyl for label pocket: 1 square 2½″ × 2½″

- Cardstock for label: 1 square 2″ × 2″

Save a Step

If you want to skip the interfacing step, use décor-weight fabric instead of quilting cotton for the lining.

CUTTING

Scraps:

Trim and press the scraps as needed.

Interfacing:

Cut 4 rectangles 6″ × 8″.

Cut 1 square 8″ × 8″.

Cardboard:

Cut 4 pieces 7¼″ × 5¼″ for the sides.

Cut 1 piece 7¼″ × 7¼″ for the bottom.

Make the Box

All seams are ¼″ unless otherwise noted.

OUTSIDE OF THE BOX

1. Make a slab of patchwork 13″ × 17″ from fabric scraps for the sides of the box (page 48). (This will be cut into the 4 side pieces later. It's easier to make a single slab, quilt it, and then cut it into 4 pieces rather than making and quilting 4 individual pieces.)

2. Make a slab of patchwork 8½″ × 8½″ from fabric scraps for the bottom of the box.

3. Layer the patchwork slabs on top of the batting pieces. *Note: You can use backing fabric if you like, but it is not necessary.*

4. Quilt as desired.

Slabs quilted with wavy lines

5. From the large quilted patchwork piece, cut 4 rectangles 6″ × 8″.

6. From the small quilted patchwork piece, cut 1 square 8″ × 8″.

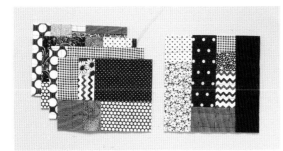

Cut pieces for box.

INSIDE OF THE BOX

1. Fuse the interfacing pieces to the lining fabric following the interfacing manufacturer's instructions.

2. Cut 4 rectangles 6″ × 8″ and 1 square 8″ × 8″.

ASSEMBLY

1. Place the 2½″ × 2½″ vinyl square in the center of a quilted side panel and sew it in place using a walking foot. Sew around 3 sides with a ⅛″ seam allowance. Leave the top open so the label can be inserted.

Sew around vinyl.

2. Check the orientation of the vinyl label sleeve to ensure that the label will insert from the top, and sew the 6″ sides of the 6″ × 8″ pieces from end to end.

3. Sew the ends together to form a square.

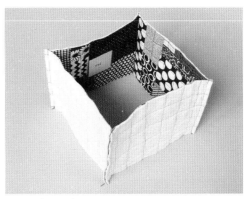

Sew ends together.

4. Pin the 8″ × 8″ square onto the bottom of the square, and sew it in place.

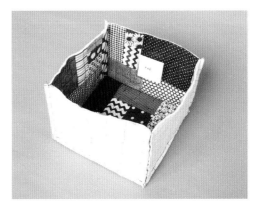

Sew bottom to sides.

5. Repeat Steps 2–4 using the interfaced pieces to make the box lining. Leave a 6″ opening in a bottom seam to allow for turning and for inserting the cardboard pieces.

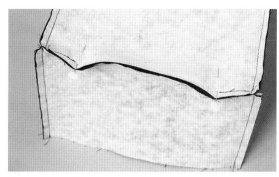

Leave opening for turning.

6. Flip the patchwork box piece right side out. Leave the lining piece wrong side out.

7. Place the patchwork piece inside the lining piece so the right sides are together.

Place quilted box inside lining.

8. Line up the edges of the box so they are even. Pin around the perimeter.

9. Sew around the top of the box.

10. Turn the box right side out, using the gap left open in the lining.

11. Roll the top seam between your fingers. Press the top seam to get a crisp edge. Make sure the hot iron doesn't touch the vinyl!

12. Topstitch around the perimeter of the box using a scant ⅛″ seam allowance.

13. Insert the cardboard pieces through the gap left open for turning. Nestle each cardboard piece in between the seams.

Insert cardboard.

All at Once

Insert all the cardboard pieces at once; then arrange them on the sides and the bottom of the box. This is easier than inserting and arranging them one at a time.

14. Sew the bottom seam either by hand or by machine.

15. Add the label and fill with scraps.

Daydreams

Made by Cheryl Arkison

finished size: 73″ × 91″

This quilt is perfect for using up the narrow strips of yardage left over from other projects. Perhaps you overbought for a project, just to make sure, but now are left with pieces that are less than 6″ from selvage to selvage. Gather those leftovers to make this quilt.

The great part about this concept is that it is easily adapted to any size of bed. The stripes cover the top of the bed, and you can adjust the plain border for the desired amount of overhang. Measure the top of your mattress. Keep the stripes on the top of the mattress only, adding or subtracting length as necessary. Then add plain borders of the same background material for the amount of overhang you want.

MATERIALS

- Stripes: 10–12 leftover selvage-to-selvage strips

- Spine: ⅜ yard accent fabric

- Background: 5 yards

- Backing: 5½ yards

- Batting: 81″ × 99″

- Binding: ¾ yard

ABOUT FABRIC SELECTION

The one strip of unicorn fabric inspired the entire quilt—my daughter was more than obsessed with unicorns for a while. I didn't want the fabric to get lost in a busy quilt, so I designed something to show off the fabric. It's a perfect complement to her stripe obsession.

I chose a color scheme that appealed to me: pink, orange, and turquoise. The brown was picked to provide high contrast to the stacked stripes. Just for fun, and because this was going in a preschooler's bedroom, I stayed away from white for the background and went with a pink shot cotton.

Use your favorite color scheme for this quilt. Pretty much anything goes—just make sure there is good contrast between the stripes and the background fabric.

CUTTING

Stripes:

The following are based on a selvage-to-selvage width of fabric.

Cut 4 strips 3″ × width of fabric.

Cut 2 strips 3½″ × width of fabric.

Cut 2 strips 4″ × width of fabric.

Cut 2 strips 4½″ × width of fabric.

Vary the length of each strip by 2″–3″.

Spine:

Cut 2 strips 4½″ × width of fabric.

Background:

Cut corresponding background strips to work with the scrap strips:

Cut 2 strips 3″ × width of fabric.

Cut 1 strip 3½″ × width of fabric.

Cut 1 strip 4″ × width of fabric.

Cut 1 strip 4½″ × width of fabric.

Cut 15 strips 4½″ × width of fabric for the background stripes.

Cut 8 strips 8½″ × width of fabric for the borders.

Binding:

Cut 9 strips 2½″ × width of fabric.

Make This Quilt

QUILT TOP

Refer to Quilt Construction Basics (pages 41–58) as needed.

1. Matching strip widths and placing right sides together, sew a background strip to each end of each scrap strip, forming a loop of fabric. Be careful not to twist the fabric strips. Press the seams toward the stripe.

Sew background to scrap strip, forming loop.

2. Fold the loop in half lengthwise, matching the ends of the stripes. From the center point of the fold, measure 27"* and mark with a pen or pencil. Using a rotary cutter, cut the strip at the mark, with the fabric still folded. Reuse the background fabric that you cut off on another stripe of a corresponding width.

Repeat for all the remaining stripes.

* If you are changing the size of the quilt, measure the width of the mattress top and divide that number in half. That will be the measurement you use in this step. You will also need to adapt the measurements in Step 3 to reflect the mattress size.

3. With right sides together, sew the 4½" background fabric strips together end to end. Press the seams to one side.

Measure out 54" lengths, mark them, and cut on the 54" marks. You should have 11 background strips.

Cut the Right Number of Background Strips

If you used more or less than the 10 stripes described here to make the quilt top the desired size, then you will need to make a different number of background strips. You should have 1 more background strip than the number of stripes.

4. Sew the scrap stripes to the background strips along the length, starting and ending with a background strip. This is the base of the quilt top.

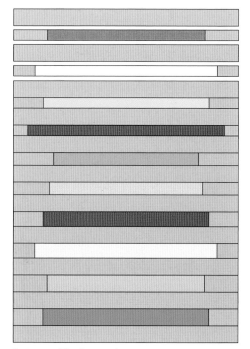

Stripes and background

5. Fold the quilt top in half, right side out. Match up the ends at the top and straighten the quilt top as needed until it is flat. Pin as needed to hold the 2 halves together.

To square up the quilt top, line up the bottom edge of a ruler along the fold, as close to the sides of the quilt top as possible. Trim only as needed to get a straight edge. Repeat on the other side.

Keep the quilt folded in half. Using the straightened sides as a guide, trim the top and bottom edges of the quilt top.

6. Measure the new width of the quilt. Hopefully you've trimmed off less than ½″, or none at all. Divide the new width by 2. Mark a line at this halved distance with a pen or pencil. (The mark will be hidden in the seam allowance, but you still don't want to use a dark or thick marker.) It should still be close to 27″. Cut along this line using a ruler and rotary cutter.

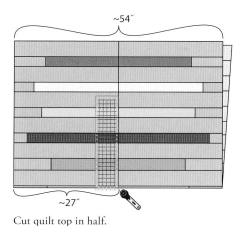

Cut quilt top in half.

Unfold the quilt top and measure the length of the quilt where you cut. Note this measurement. You will need it for the next step and when cutting borders.

7. With right sides together, sew the 2 pieces of accent fabric together to make the spine. Press.

Measure and mark the spine to the same length as you measured the quilt top in Step 6. Cut.

With right sides together, sew the spine in between the 2 halves of the quilt top. Press toward the spine.

8. Measure the width of the quilt top. Note this measurement. You will need it in Step 10, cutting borders.

9. With right sides together, sew the 8½″-wide background strips together end to end. Press the seams to one side. You should have 1 long strip to cut the borders from.

10. Measure and mark the length of the background strips needed for the width. Use the measurement from Step 8. Cut 2 pieces of background strip for the top and bottom. With right sides together, sew the top and bottom border to the quilt top. Press.

11. Measure the length of the quilt top (including the top and bottom borders). Cut 2 strips to length from the remaining 8½″ background strips. With right sides together, sew the side borders to the quilt top through the middle. Press.

12. When the quilt top is assembled, sew a straight or zigzag stitch ⅛″ in from the outside edge of the quilt. This will prevent the seams from splitting during handling before it is quilted.

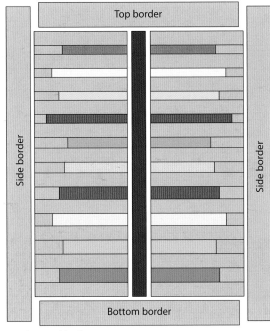

Quilt assembly diagram

BACKING, QUILTING, AND FINISHING

Refer to Turning the Pieced Top into a Quilt (pages 50–57) as needed.

1. Piece the backing fabric into a rectangle 81″ × 99″. Press.

2. Layer the backing fabric, batting, and quilt top. Baste the quilt.

3. Quilt as desired.

4. Trim the excess batting and backing from the edge of the quilt.

5. Attach the binding by machine and stitch it down with your preferred method.

MAKE IT YOURS

- Piece the large colored stripes from scraps. Make up a color-block stripe or piece strips vertically into a long chain, as in *Candy Coated* (page 86).

- Play around with the background fabric, but make sure there is a strong contrast with the stripes.

- Remove the spine or add more to change the overall design.

- Pick a busy background fabric and a calmer choice for the stripes.

ABOUT THE QUILTING

Your quilting will be quite obvious on this quilt, with the all-solid or nearly solid background. Pick a thread that coordinates with the background. Pick a pattern that you don't mind seeing a lot of. I chose loops to contrast with the sharp corners of the stripes. I did, however, echo the notion of stripes in the placement of the loop pattern.

Splash

Made by Amanda Jean Nyberg

finished size: 52″ × 68″

This quilt was inspired by the look of the popular wonky Log Cabin block. It doesn't come together like a Log Cabin; rather, it uses the slab technique (page 48) to turn scraps into fabric. Sewn together, those slabs mimic a single Log Cabin block. What a fun way to celebrate your favorite color combination.

MATERIALS

- Orange scraps

- Aqua scraps

- 4 white scrap strips at least 3″ × 18″ or 1 white fat quarter

- Backing: 3½ yards

- Batting: 60″ × 76″

- Binding: ⅔ yard

CUTTING

White:

Cut 4 strips 3″ × 18″.

Binding:

Cut 7 strips 2½″ × width of fabric.

ABOUT FABRIC SELECTION

Most of the fabrics used in this quilt are medium values. I used some lights in larger doses and used the darks sparingly as highlights.

Make This Quilt

QUILT TOP

Refer to Quilt Construction Basics (pages 41–58) as needed.

1. Make a slab 13½" × 15" from orange scraps (page 48).

2. Sew the white strips to the 15" sides of the orange block. Press and trim the overhanging ends of white. Sew the remaining white strips to the remaining 2 sides of the orange block. Press and trim off the ends.

Trim the block to 16" × 17¼". Feel free to tip the block to make it a little bit wonky as you trim. Label it A.

3. From the aqua scraps, make slabs in the following sizes:

16" × 11¾"; label B	4" × 49½"; label H
16" × 26¾"; label C	3½" × 58¼"; label I
20¼" × 28¼"; label D	3½" × 52½"; label J
20¼" × 27"; label E	5¾" × 52½"; label K
14¼" × 26¼"; label F	2½" × 52½"; label L
14¼" × 29"; label G	

Press each slab well.

4. Arrange the blocks as shown in the quilt assembly diagram (below). With right sides together, sew the blocks together as described below.

Sew C to A.

Sew CA to B.

Sew D to E.

Sew F to G.

Sew DE to CAB.

Sew DECAB to FG.

Sew DECABFG to H.

Sew DECABFGH to I.

Sew J to K.

Sew DECABFGHI to JK.

Sew DECABFGHIJK to L.

5. When the quilt top is assembled, sew a straight or zigzag stitch ⅛″ in from the outside edge of the quilt. This will prevent the seams from splitting during handling before it is quilted.

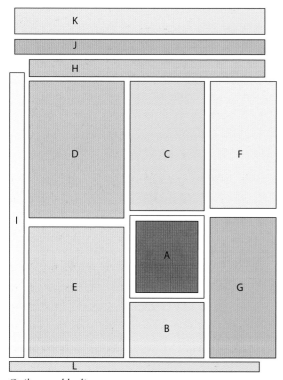

Quilt assembly diagram

BACKING, QUILTING, AND FINISHING

Refer to Turning the Pieced Top into a Quilt (pages 50–57) as needed.

1. Piece the backing fabric into a rectangle 60″ × 76″. Press.

2. Layer the backing fabric, batting, and quilt top. Baste the quilt.

3. Quilt as desired.

4. Trim the excess batting and backing from the edge of the quilt.

5. Attach the binding by machine and stitch it down with your preferred method.

MAKE IT YOURS

- Use your favorite two-color combination to make this quilt; consider brown and aqua, gray and yellow, red and aqua, or pink and green.

- Use a red and green color scheme to make a modern Christmas quilt.

- Make the orange block smaller and make three rather than one. Align the blocks vertically and place them slightly off-center.

- Use the same color scheme throughout all the blocks to make a monochromatic quilt.

ABOUT THE QUILTING

Choosing a single thread color to quilt with was difficult, so I decided to quilt the elements of this piece separately and matched the thread color accordingly.

I used a walking foot to stitch in-the-ditch around the white strips to stabilize the strips and the orange block. In the orange square, I quilted several nearly parallel horizontal lines. In the white strips, I used a free-motion foot to add pebble quilting. I quilted the aqua section by making wavy interlocking lines with a walking foot.

Grass

Made by Cheryl Arkison

finished size: 68″ × 68″

Once you start following the blogs of many modern quilters, popular or not, you will soon be overwhelmed by variations on a theme. Start with wonky Log Cabin or similar types of blocks and set them with white sashing. I'm not knocking these quilts—they're easy, they're quick, and they can be real stunners—but a girl gets tired of seeing the same thing all the time! So I set out to make a quilt in direct opposition. This quilt combines plain white blocks with pieced sashing. As a result, the quilting is on display. Take that, white sashing!

This quilt was also inspired by grass. We were landscaping and I stared out my window at mountains of dirt. Thankfully, I have an imagination and could just picture the patio that we would eventually put in. Simple square stones set in a grid, with a sashing of grass in between the stones. *Grass* is the result of that bit of daydreaming.

MATERIALS

- White: 2¼ yards or assortment of large scraps or leftovers

- Mix of lights, mediums, and darks: 80 strips at least 3″ × 14″ and 100 snippets

- Backing: 4¼ yards

- Batting: 76″ × 76″

- Binding: ¾ yard

CUTTING

White:

Cut 16 squares 12½″ × 12½″.

Snippets and strips:

Trim the scraps to yield the approximate amounts required (see Materials, above). Don't worry about the sizes being exact or perfect at this point.

Binding:

Cut 8 strips 2½″ × width of fabric.

It's Okay If You Prefer Precision Piecing

If you aren't comfortable with wonky blocks, cut the strips to 2½″ × 12½″ and the snippets to 2½″ × 2½″ squares.

ABOUT FABRIC SELECTION

This quilt is particularly bold when made using just one color for the pieced sashing. The interest in this monochromatic look comes from using fabrics with different values and tones. Mix around the lights and darks, add in some fabrics with more gray, and then add some that are bright with white tones.

If you are set on making a two-color sashing, then choose colors that go well together, such as yellow and green or red and purple, or high-contrast colors such as orange and aqua.

The main blocks look best in white (in the antisashing spirit) or a neutral. Mix up a number of white-on-whites, go for a solid white, or piece slabs (page 48).

Make This Quilt

QUILT TOP

Refer to Quilt Construction Basics (pages 41–58) as needed.

1. Sort the fabric strips and snippets into lights and darks. If you are unsure about where a fabric goes, start a new pile and call those pieces medium. Set the piles next to your sewing machine, within easy reach.

2. With right sides together, sew a light strip and a dark strip together. Don't worry if they aren't the exact same length, as you'll trim them later. Continue to sew strips together in pairs. Sometimes you will sew together lights with mediums and sometimes mediums with darks. Make 40 pairs of strips.

3. Press the sashing set strip pairs, either with the seams open or with the seam allowances toward the dark.

4. Trim each sashing set to 4½″ × 12½″—be as wonky as you feel comfortable being. The nice thing about going wonky is that it makes use of odd-sized strings without wasting as much fabric. Vary the wonkiness by rotating your ruler, ensuring that you still have enough fabric for the required trimmed size. Not comfortable with being a bit off-kilter? That's okay too. Line up the seam-line on the 2¼″ line.

Trim sashing sets.

5. The corner pieces of the sashing are essentially simple four-patch units. With right sides together, sew together a light snippet with a dark snippet. Continue to sew all the snippets together in pairs. Sometimes you will sew together lights with mediums and sometimes mediums with darks. Make 50 pairs.

6. Press the seam allowances in the pairs toward the dark fabric.

7. Make four-patches from the pairs. Make sure you are sewing lights to darks as you assemble the pairs with right sides together. Be sure that when sewn together they will be at least 4½″ × 4½″. Sew all the pairs together, being careful to line up the center seams. If you've pressed the seam allowance in each pair toward the dark snippet, lining the pairs up at the seams should be easy because the seams will nest. Make 25 four-patches.

> ### Make Sure Your Pieced Four-Patch Is Big Enough
>
> Keep a ruler or cardboard template that is cut to the trimmed block size close by while you sew. You can compare the blocks as you match pieces and sew. This saves a lot of wasted blocks when it comes time to trim.

8. Press the squares with the seams open or to one side.

9. Trim each rough square to 4½″ × 4½″. Again, get as wonky as you want to be.

Trim four-patches.

10. Arrange all the pieces according to the quilt assembly diagram. Start with the white squares. In the upper left corner, place a four-patch square with the light square in the outermost corner. In the sashing spots next to it, place sashing sets with the dark color against the white square. The next corner spot will also have the light against the white. For the next white square this will be reversed, with the dark next to the white block. Continue in this manner until everything is placed.

If you are making a 2-color sashing, the same layout principles apply, but alternate the colors in the layout rather than the values.

Reference Your Layout

Before I start piecing a top I like to take a picture of it with my digital camera. This way I have a reference in case I get mixed up at any point. I also like to pin something, like a scrap of fabric in a contrasting color, in the top left corner as a point of reference.

11. When you are satisfied with the layout, begin sewing. With right sides together, sew the top left four-patch to the horizontal sashing piece to the right of it. Without breaking the thread, sew the leftmost vertical sashing piece to the adjacent white block. Continue chain piecing down through the rows, alternately adding the leftmost four-patches to the horizontal sashing pieces and the leftmost vertical sashing pieces to the white blocks, until you have sewn together the first two columns of sub-units. Do not break the thread and do not stitch the horizontal seams.

12. Add the third column of four-patches and vertical sashing to the already-stitched pairs of sub-units, chain piecing down through the rows as before. Assemble the remainder of the quilt top in this manner.

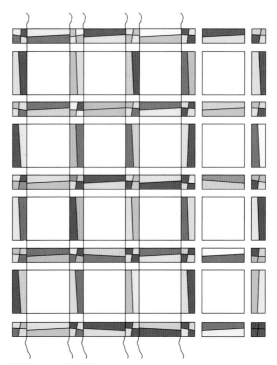

Quilt assembly diagram

13. I recommend pressing toward the horizontal sashing in the 4½″ rows and toward the vertical sashing in the 12½″ rows. This will ensure that the white blocks do not have a dark seam allowance showing through, and the finished quilt will lie smooth.

Manage Your Pressing Direction

It might seem more intuitive to sew together the rows by size—the 4½″ rows and the 12½″ rows. But by chain piecing the rows as directed it is easier to keep track of pressing directions.

14. After the rows are sewn together and pressed, pin them together at the intersections of all the white blocks. Sew the rows together. Press all the rows toward the sashing sections.

15. When the quilt top is assembled, sew a straight or zigzag stitch ⅛″ in from the outside edge of the quilt. This will prevent the seams from splitting during handling until it is quilted.

MAKE IT YOURS

- Instead of squares for the center blocks, try rectangles.

- Create the sashing strips with smaller strips and place them on the horizontal, not the vertical, when you sew them together—similar to a coin quilt construction. You can use the shorter strips to create a multicolor or monochromatic sashing.

- Create the sashing strips or the white blocks using the slab technique (page 48).

- Pick a different-color solid for the center blocks.

BACKING, QUILTING, AND FINISHING

Refer to Turning the Pieced Top into a Quilt (pages 50–57) as needed.

1. Piece the backing fabric into a square 76″ × 76″. Press.

2. Layer the backing fabric, batting, and quilt top. Baste the quilt.

3. Quilt as desired.

4. Trim the excess batting and backing from the edge of the quilt.

5. Attach the binding by machine and stitch it down with your preferred method.

ABOUT THE QUILTING

With such a sharp contrast between the sashing and the white blocks, thread choice becomes very important. You can choose to quilt the sashing and the white blocks separately, or showcase your quilting with a high-contrast thread. Your quilting will be quite visible on the white sections in particular. Don't let this scare you. Jump in with a bold pattern. The quilting here is a free-motion design that mimics blades of grass.

Scrapper's Delight

Made by Amanda Jean Nyberg

block size: 12″ × 12″

finished size: 72″ × 72″

The front of this quilt is made from 100 percent scraps. To be honest, this one was very challenging for me. I so wanted to fall back on my old standby—white sashing—to separate the 24″ squares. I struggled for days to get all the scraps to mesh. The quilt is quite busy, but it was great to challenge myself to use just scraps, with no sashing whatsoever. I'm so glad I did—this has turned into one of my very favorites!

The quilt was named by Cheryl. When she saw it completed, she instantly thought *Scrapper's Delight*. Just a little nod to her old-school rap influences.

MATERIALS

- Multicolor: Strings and snippets 1″–13″ in length, in various widths

- Backing: 4½ yards

- Batting: 80″ × 80″

- Binding: ¾ yard

- 12½″ × 12½″ square ruler

CUTTING

Binding:

Cut 9 strips 2½″ × width of fabric.

ABOUT FABRIC SELECTION

I used a large variety of colors and prints. Most fabrics are medium value, but some lights and a few darks are sprinkled throughout. Doing so means that the quilt doesn't fall flat. Using all medium values would lose interest. When making the individual blocks, you can use a multicolored fabric or two to guide the color choices for the rest of the block.

Make This Quilt

QUILT TOP

Refer to Quilt Construction Basics (pages 41–58) as needed.

1. Start with a snippet anywhere from 1″ × 1″ to 2″ × 2″. It can be a square or a rectangle. Sew another snippet or a string to it, right sides together. Press the seam away from the center block. Trim the excess ends.

2. With right sides together, sew a string to the adjacent side. Press the seam away from the center block. Trim off the excess ends. When constructing the blocks, try to add similar-width strips to each side in order to maintain a mostly square shape during construction.

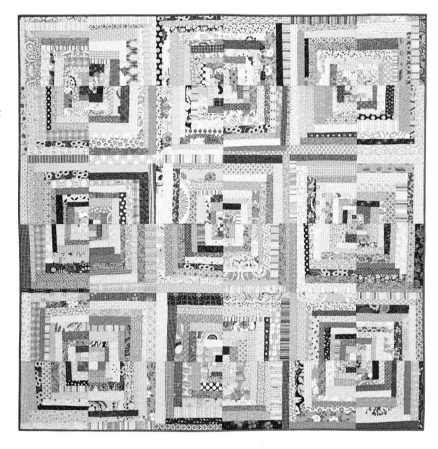

Use a Short Stitch Length

Sew with a stitch length of no more than a 2, as the blocks are cut down after assembly. Handle them carefully and as little as possible to prevent seams from splitting.

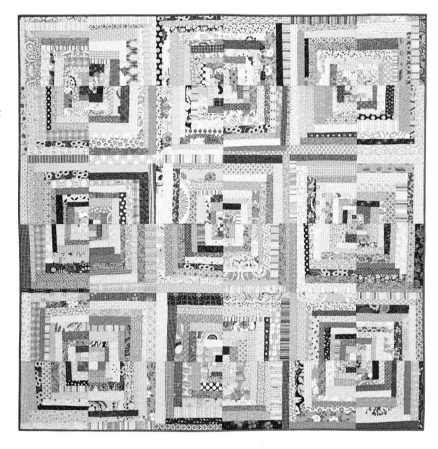

3. Keep adding strips to just the 2 sides. Periodically place the 12½″ × 12½″ ruler over the block to make sure that it is staying relatively square during the piecing process. Squaring the block up a few times during the block construction is another option for maintaining the shape as you sew. Continue until the block is slightly larger than 12½″ × 12½″. Press well. Use starch if necessary to keep the block flat (page 46).

Block diagram

Finish with Thick Strips

Use pieces at least 2″ wide for the final strips. This allows you to trim the block without leaving thin slivers on the outside edges.

4. Make 36 blocks.

5. Use the ruler to trim each block to 12½″ × 12½″.

6. Arrange the blocks according to the quilt assembly diagram.

7. Sew the blocks into rows. Press. Sew the rows together to complete the quilt top. Press.

8. When the quilt top is assembled, sew a straight or zigzag stitch ⅛″ in from the outside edge of the quilt. This will prevent the seams from splitting during handling before it is quilted.

Quilt assembly diagram

BACKING, QUILTING, AND FINISHING

Refer to Turning the Pieced Top into a Quilt (pages 50–57) as needed.

1. Piece the backing fabric into a square 80″ × 80″. Press.

2. Layer the backing fabric, batting, and quilt top. Baste the quilt.

3. Quilt as desired.

4. Trim the excess batting and backing from the edge of the quilt.

5. Attach the binding by machine and stitch it down with your preferred method.

MAKE IT YOURS

* Arrange the blocks so they face in one direction only, rather than having them facing together in groups of four.

* Make some 6½″ × 6½″ blocks in the same manner. Use sets of four small blocks to replace random 12½″ × 12½″ blocks throughout the quilt.

* Make all the blocks half the size to make it a baby quilt instead of a throw. This would yield a 36″ × 36″ quilt.

ABOUT THE QUILTING

The quilting on this piece takes a backseat to the busy layout, and that's the way it should be. I did an allover free-motion swirl with a thin natural-colored thread. This adds plenty of texture to the quilt without competing with the design of the blocks.

Candy Coated

Made by Amanda Jean Nyberg

finished size: 63½″ × 88″

If your scraps are anything like mine, you always seem to have a basket full of strings. This quilt is a good way to start making a serious dent in the basket. The beauty of this quilt is that it uses different lengths of strings. Start by piecing together the longest strings first. Use the leftovers from the long strings to piece the shorter strings.

MATERIALS

- Strings and strips in 3 colorways: roughly 630, depending on widths

- Backing: 5½ yards

- Batting: 72″ × 96″

- Binding: ¾ yard

CUTTING

Strings and strips:

40–50 strips about 11″	40–50 strips about 7″
40–50 strips about 10½″	80–100 strips about 6″
40–50 strips about 9″	40–50 strips about 5½″
120–150 strips about 8½″	80–100 strips about 5″
40–50 strips about 8″	40–50 strips about 3½″

Binding:

Cut 8 strips 2½″ × width of fabric.

ABOUT FABRIC SELECTION

I wanted to make a soft quilt with just a few pops of color. Varying the amounts of darks and lights would dramatically change the look of this quilt.

Make This Quilt

QUILT TOP

*Refer to Quilt Construction Basics
(pages 41–58) as needed.*

1. With right sides together, sew several
11″ strings together side by side. Press the seams
to one side. Work in sections no longer than your
ruler. Trim each section to 10½″ high. Trim the
ends of each section to a 90° angle.

2. For each row, make several sections of
various widths. The rows are worked in sections
because it is much easier to trim individual sections than it is to trim a 64″-wide row. Vary the
widths of the sections as you work on them.
If you made each section exactly 20″ wide, for
example, straight vertical lines would emerge
on the quilt top when you sewed all the rows
together. Connect the sections together until
each is 64″ wide.

3. Make the rest of the rows for the quilt
according to the directions in Steps 1 and 2.
Follow the list below for the number and size
of rows to be completed.

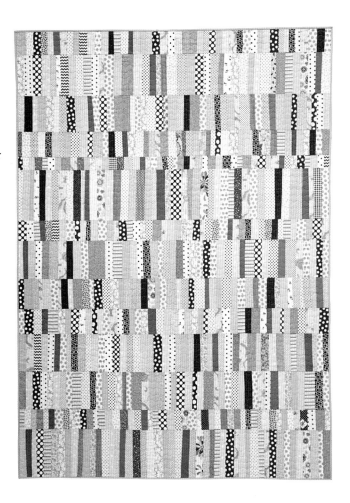

Use the 10½″-long strips to
make a row 10″ × 64″. Make 1.

Use the 9″-long strips to make
a row 8½″ × 64″. Make 1.

Use the 8½″-long strips to
make a row 8″ × 64″. Make 3.

Use the 8″-long strips to make
a row 7½″ × 64″. Make 1.

Use the 7″-long strips to make
a row 6½″ × 64″. Make 1.

Use the 6″-long strips to make
a row 5½″ × 64″. Make 2.

Use the 5½″-long strips to
make a row 5″ × 64″. Make 1.

Use the 5″-long strips to make
a row 4½″ × 64″. Make 2.

Use the 3½″-long strips to
make a row 3″ × 64″. Make 1.

Mark a Length on the Floor

It's not easy to measure a 64″ strip on a standard-size cutting mat. My solution was to measure and mark a 64″ length on my hardwood floor. (I made sure the marks were only temporary.) Depending on your flooring, something low tack such as painter's tape could work well. This makes it much easier to measure the rows and gauge the length of the rows as you are working on them.

Pin Liberally When Sewing Together Rows

The number of seams makes the rows very stretchy. This is why pinning at this stage is so important. But on the bright side, this also allows you to ease the rows together when sewing.

4. Arrange the rows according to the quilt assembly diagram.

5. Sew the rows together. Press the seams to one side.

6. When the quilt top is assembled, sew a straight or zigzag stitch ⅛″ in from the outside edge of the quilt. This will prevent the seams from splitting during handling before it is quilted.

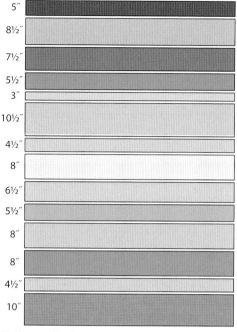

Quilt assembly diagram

BACKING, QUILTING, AND FINISHING

Refer to Turning the Pieced Top into a Quilt (pages 50–57) as needed.

1. Piece the backing fabric into a rectangle 72″ × 96″. Press.

2. Layer the backing fabric, batting, and quilt top. Baste the quilt.

3. Quilt as desired.

4. Trim the excess batting and backing from the edge of the quilt.

5. Attach the binding by machine and stitch it down with your preferred method.

ABOUT THE QUILTING

This was quilted with horizontal wavy lines about 1″–2″ apart in a light gray thread. I used a free-motion quilting technique to achieve this. Many machines on the market have the capability of making similar, but smaller-scale, stitching.

MAKE IT YOURS

- Mix up the heights of the rows according to the scraps you have on hand.

- Make each row wider if you want to make a full-size quilt.

- Tip a few sections of strings on their sides within the rows.

- Arrange all the rows vertically, making a free-form coin quilt.

- If you want to break up the rows of vertical stripes, try inserting a narrow horizontal band of a single color between the rows.

Candy Coated

Nap Like an Egyptian

Made by Cheryl Arkison

block size: 9″ equilateral triangle block

finished size: 54″ × 38″

MATERIALS

- Strings and strips in a single color for triangle logs: Approximately 275 strips 3″–9″ long and 1″–2″ wide

- Background: 3¼ yards (1½ yards light and 1¾ yards dark)

- Backing: 2⅝ yards

- Batting: 62″ × 46″

- Binding: ½ yard

- Equilateral triangle template or 60° triangle ruler*

You can purchase these rulers from many retailers. (I like the Marti Michell one.) Don't worry if you don't have a ruler with 9″ sides. Simply use the same one for all the triangles and add or subtract rows as necessary to achieve the desired final size. Otherwise, see Make Your Own Triangle Template (page 92) for instructions on how to easily make your own without any special tools.

Modern quilt design is inherently tied to traditional quilting. Rather than discarding the techniques of old, this quilt adapts and updates them. The blocks in this quilt are put together exactly like traditional Log Cabin blocks, except that the first piece is a triangle, not a square. It's a simple update with dramatic results.

Each triangle block is pieced improvisationally. Likewise, the quilt is the result of improvisation. My original intention was to have an all-light background. Unfortunately, halfway through piecing the blocks it became clear that I wasn't going to have enough of the fabric, and no more would be available in time. After making more blocks with the darker background and playing with the layout, this is the result. It was rather fitting that it was pieced as the 2011 revolution in Egypt played out. A little unconscious inspiration, perhaps?

ABOUT FABRIC SELECTION

We believe that this quilt sings when the colored logs are featured, so a high contrast between the background fabric and the featured logs is needed, which will allow the triangle shape to stand out. If in doubt about the contrast, take a photo of the fabrics and look at it in black and white—the differences between them should be obvious.

CUTTING

Strings and strips:

Trim the strings and strips to the desired width.

Background:

You will make 3 shapes from the background fabric; 2 will be made from the dark fabric.

Dark

Cut 2 strips 5½″ × width of fabric. Layer the strips together, wrong sides facing and cut edges even. Align the vertical centerline of the triangle ruler (or template) with the cut edge of the layered fabric strips. Shift the ruler so that the ¼″ seam allowance guide is lined up with the cut edge of the strip. (Take care as you shift away from the centerline that you are *adding* a seam allowance and not removing it.) Cut out a half–equilateral triangle. Rotate the ruler 180°. Align its vertical centerline along the other side of the strip, line the seam allowance guide up with the cut edge, and cut another half–equilateral triangle. Cut 5 pairs of triangles this way. These are the setting triangles for the side edges of the quilt. By cutting them from layered fabric with the wrong sides facing, you have cut the half–equilateral triangle and its reverse at the same time.

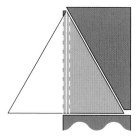

Cut the remainder into strips varying between 2″ and 3″ × width of fabric.

Cut 30 triangles from 2 of the strips. They do not need to be precisely measured, but aim for roughly equilateral triangles for the centers of the log cabins.

Light

Cut into strips varying between 2″ and 3″ × width of fabric.

Cut 25 triangles from 2 of the strips. They do not need to be precisely measured, but aim for roughly equilateral triangles for the centers of the log cabins.

Binding:

Cut 5 strips 2½″ × width of fabric.

Make This Quilt

MAKE YOUR OWN TRIANGLE TEMPLATE

Draw a line 9″ long. At the 4½″ mark, draw a perpendicular line at least 8″ long.

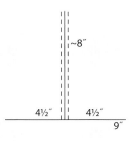

From one end of the first line, measure 9″ up to the line drawn down the center. Draw that line. Repeat on the other side. Please note that this is 9″ for the length of that outside line, not the 9″ height of the centerline. Mark a dotted line ¼″ from the centerline on either side. These are the seam allowance guides. Using this triangle, create a template out of template plastic or cardboard, and transfer all the markings.

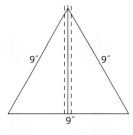

QUILT TOP

Refer to Quilt Construction Basics (pages 41–58) as needed.

1. Work in batches of 5 blocks at a time, and stick with 1 background color per batch. With right sides together, sew together a center triangle and a triangle log strip. Make sure that the strip overhangs each end of the triangle by at least 1″. Chain piece the rest of the batch, sewing a strip to the center triangle. Press toward the strip.

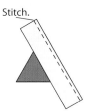

Sew log strip to center triangle.

Chain Piecing

Chain piecing saves time and thread. Sew one seam; then sew a few stitches of nothing and immediately feed in the next pieces to start sewing the next seam. Do this instead of starting and stopping with each new seam to be sewn as you piece blocks together. Clip the chains apart as you advance through the piecing stages.

Make Logs Long Enough

Before you sew down any strips, make sure that when pressed they cover the corners fully. Hold the strip, right side up, next to the existing block to check the fit. Then flip it right sides together to sew. You will have excess fabric, but it can be trimmed off afterward.

2. Rotate the triangle so that the strip is on the left-hand side of the center triangle. With right sides together, sew a second strip to the center triangle, making sure there is a minimum 1″ overhang at the ends. Trim the seam allowance to ¼″, including the overhang from the previous strip. Press toward the strip.

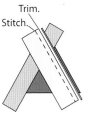

Sew second log to center triangle.

3. Add the third strip in the same manner.

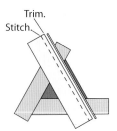

Add third strip.

4. Repeat Steps 1–3 to add a round of logs made from the background fabric using the same color as the center triangle. Always trim the seam allowance after sewing each strip and press toward the colored strip, not the background.

Test against your ruler or template. Finished blocks should measure at least 9″ on all sides. Add another log of background fabric, as necessary.

5. When all the blocks in the batch are at least 9″ on all sides, press them well and trim them to size with your ruler or template.

6. Make 55 blocks total—25 blocks with the light background and 30 with the dark background.

7. Referring to the quilt assembly diagram as needed, arrange all the light background blocks. Start with the bottom row. Place 9 blocks across the bottom, alternating the direction of the block. The row above should have 7 blocks, then 5, then 3, then 1.

Add the dark background blocks around the outside of the pyramid. The bottom of the pyramid will be framed with 1 dark background block on each side. Moving up the pyramid you will add 2, 3, 4, and then 5 blocks to each side. Each row should have 11 blocks in total. Place a setting triangle at the end of each row.

8. With right sides together, sew the blocks together to make rows. Press well and then sew the rows together. Press again.

Quilt assembly diagram

9. When the quilt top is assembled, sew a straight or zigzag stitch ⅛″ in from the outside edge of the quilt. This will prevent the seams from splitting during handling before it is quilted.

BACKING, QUILTING, AND FINISHING

Refer to Turning the Pieced Top into a Quilt (pages 50–57) as needed.

1. Piece the backing fabric into a rectangle 62″ × 46″. Press.

2. Layer the backing fabric, batting, and quilt top. Baste the quilt.

3. Quilt as desired.

4. Trim the excess batting and backing from the edge of the quilt.

5. Attach the binding by machine and stitch it down with your preferred method.

ABOUT THE QUILTING

There are a lot of seams in this quilt and they go in every direction. This would make stippling a challenge. I chose an allover random line look. It accentuates the graphic nature of the quilt and is easy to manage. You might prefer to outline the logs, making them really stand out.

MAKE IT YOURS

- Exchange the light and dark areas.

- Pick a single-color background and use multicolored scraps for the featured logs (see page 15).

- Add rows and columns to increase the size of the quilt.

- Change the size of the triangles overall. Or make one large triangle the size of four put together.

- Pick a colored background and use white feature logs. Perfect for using leftover sashing strips!

Sunday Morning

Made by Cheryl Arkison

block size: 10″ × 10″

finished size: 80″ × 90″

MATERIALS

- Scraps: 450 strips approximately 1″–3″ × 8½″ and 72 strips approximately 3″ × 11″

- Backing: 7½ yards

- Batting: 88″ × 98″

- Binding: ¾ yard

CUTTING

Strips:

Trim the strips to size if the pieces are longer or wider.

If you are more comfortable with precision piecing, cut horizontal strips 2½″ × 8½″ and vertical strips 3″ × 11″.

Binding:

Cut 9 strips 2½″ × width of fabric.

So many modern quilt fabrics are bold: saturated colors, cutesy images, or interesting graphics. They all pair well with whites or neutrals. But hidden among the bolds and brights are what are often called low-volume fabrics. These have predominantly white, light, or neutral backgrounds with interesting designs. The scale of the fabric design varies, but the overall effect is softer and quieter than that of most modern fabrics. Smaller-scale prints, reminiscent of Grand-mother's calicoes, mix well with the large-scale graphic prints for a stunning effect.

ABOUT FABRIC SELECTION

Your fabric choices will make this a bold or soft quilt. With low-volume fabrics the overall effect is somewhat ethereal. At home in a very modern bedroom, this quilt is sunshine and light combined with the comfort of a quilt. Perfect for lazy Sunday mornings.

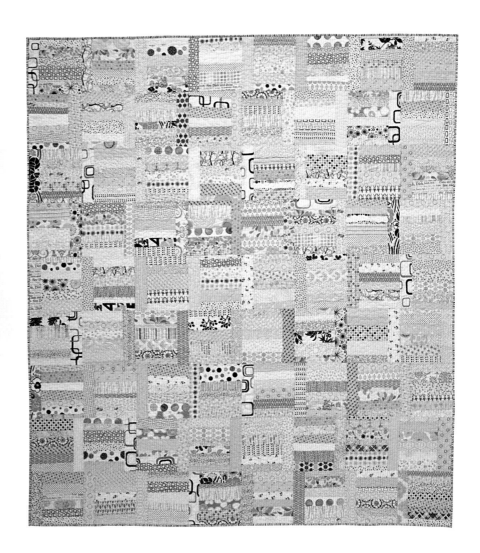

Make This Quilt

QUILT TOP

Refer to Quilt Construction Basics (pages 41–58) as needed.

1. Organize the strips into 2 piles. The larger pile, with the 8½″-long strips, will make all the horizontal pieces of the blocks. The smaller pile will be the longer 11″-long strips. Set aside the 11″-long strips for the time being.

Grab a large paper shopping bag, plastic bin, or cardboard box. Throw in all the 8½″-long strips and mix them up well. You will be putting the blocks together by simply grabbing strips out of the bag as you go.

2. Take 2 strips from the bag. Place them right sides together and sew them together along a long side. Continue to sew pairs together until you are about ¾ of the way through the strips.

3. Press all the seam allowances either to one side or open, whichever you prefer.

4. Sew 1 pair to another until you've gone through approximately two-thirds of the pairs. Press again, the same way you initially pressed the pairs.

5. The height of the block needs to be 10½″. Measure the height of the strip set and sew on either a single strip or another pair—whichever is needed to reach 10½″. Continue to sew strips together, using all the 8½″ strips until you reach the desired number of blocks. The pictured quilt has 72 blocks.

If you've gone the route of precision piecing, use 5 horizontal strips to make the correct finished height.

6. Press all the blocks well.

> ## Keep Fabric Placement in Mind with Directional Fabrics
>
> If you are using fabrics with a definite top and bottom, choose which side you will be adding the vertical strip to before you begin sewing. Also, when laying out the quilt, pay attention to which direction the fabric is facing. This way you can be sure that directional prints will always be viewed correctly.

7. Using a ruler and rotary cutter, trim a side of the strip set so it is straight.

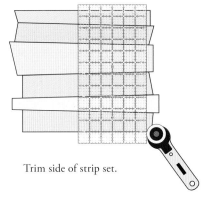

Trim side of strip set.

8. Pull out the 11″ strips. With right sides together, sew an 11″-long strip to the trimmed side of each block. Press toward the 11″ strip.

9. Trim each block to 10½″ × 10½″. To ensure consistency, line up your ruler with the vertical seam on the block. Make the first trim cut 2½″ away from that seam on the vertical side. Trim the rest of the block based on that first cut.

10. Referring to the quilt assembly diagram, arrange the blocks. By row, alternate the side of the block where the vertical strip is placed.

11. Assemble the quilt top. With right sides together, sew the blocks together into rows. Press to the vertical strip. Pin and sew the rows together. Press.

Use Labels to Keep Rows in Order

Label each row with a piece of tape or pin a small piece of paper to the top left corner of the left block in each row (1-2-3-4-5, and so on). Keep these on until the entire top is sewn together. It will ensure that your blocks stay in the order you want them.

12. When the quilt top is assembled, sew a straight or zigzag stitch ⅛″ in from the outside edge of the quilt. This will prevent the seams from splitting during handling before it is quilted.

Quilt assembly diagram

Change the Size

The size of the quilt is easily varied by changing the number of blocks used. With a 10″ × 10″ finished block, the up- or down-sizing is easy.

BACKING, QUILTING, AND FINISHING

Refer to Turning the Pieced Top into a Quilt (pages 50–57) as needed.

1. Piece the backing fabric into a rectangle 88″ × 98″. Press.

2. Layer the backing fabric, batting, and quilt top. Baste the quilt.

3. Quilt as desired.

4. Trim the excess batting and backing from the edge of the quilt.

5. Attach the binding by machine and stitch it down with your preferred method.

MAKE IT YOURS

- Instead of using low-volume fabrics, use bold, more saturated colors. You can create a vibrant multicolored quilt by making individual blocks in a single colorway.

- Make a themed quilt. For an easy seasonal quilt, pick a theme such as Halloween or Christmas.

- Make each block a rainbow in itself, moving from one color to the next, or from light to dark values of a single color, with each strip.

- Use the same fabric for each vertical piece.

- Alternate the layout of the blocks to create lines, stripes, or shapes.

ABOUT THE QUILTING

To contrast with all the straight lines, I chose a curvy quilting pattern. The quilt is covered with flowers of many sizes, from 2″ in diameter to 20″. There aren't as many seams in this quilt as there are in some of our slab quilts, so it is much easier to tackle this free-motion design. I wish you could feel this quilt—the texture is amazing!

The Missing U

Made by Cheryl Arkison

block size: 15″ × 15″

finished size: 75″ × 75″

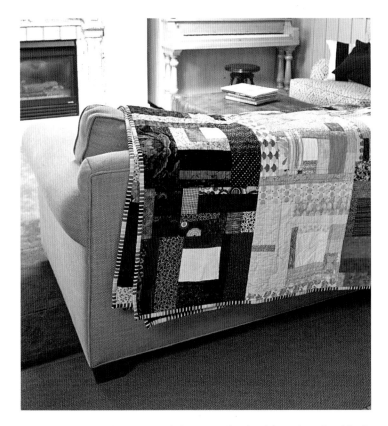

MATERIALS

- Scraps, sorted by color and value, in at least 5 different colors

- Assorted white scraps

- Backing: 4⅝ yards

- Batting: 83″ × 83″

- Binding: ¾ yard

CUTTING

Colored scraps:

Trim as necessary to prepare for slab construction (page 48).

White scraps:

Cut 25 squares or rectangles, 2″–6″ × 2″–6″.

Binding:

Cut 8 strips 2½″ × width of fabric.

This is the quilt that inspired the entire book. I'd made a few blocks and shared the photos with Amanda Jean. She got excited by the idea and offered to make a few blocks from her own scraps to contribute to the quilt. This marked the beginning of the collaboration of this book. Finished at a larger size, the blocks are great for such a bold design. The best part about this project, though, is that you can make the blocks any size you want and make as many you want. You could even ask your friends to cocntribute to your quilt.

As a Canadian I struggled at times while writing this book. I was forever writing *colour* and *favourite.* Because color was the key to this quilt, I named it after my missing U in the word *color* itself.

ABOUT FABRIC SELECTION

While color is obviously central to these blocks, value is also important. In this quilt each color has both light blocks and dark blocks, such as dark green and light green, dark red and pink, and so on. Notice that the white scrap stands out most when used in blocks of darker colors. If you mix up all the values of each color, rather than making blocks that are primarily dark or primarily light, the white scrap will tend to get lost. If you like, you can leave out the white scrap altogether and mix the values as you choose.

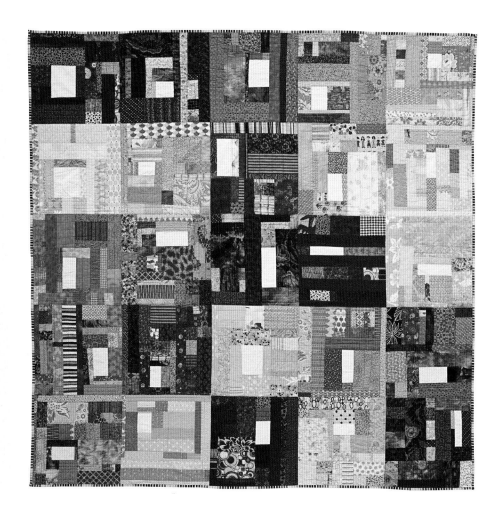

Make This Quilt

QUILT TOP

Refer to Quilt Construction Basics (pages 41–58) as needed.

1. Starting with a white scrap, build out a slab in a single color. Make sure that the white scrap is surrounded by color on all 4 sides—other than that, it doesn't matter exactly where in the block the white scrap ends up. Continue until the block measures just larger than 15½″ × 15½″. Trim the block to 15½″ × 15½″.

2. Sew around the perimeter about ⅛″ in from the edge using a small zigzag or straight stitch. This stitching keeps the seams of the trimmed block from splitting and will be contained in the seam allowance when the blocks are pieced together.

3. Repeat to make 25 unique blocks. If you want to have the same layout as the pictured quilt, you need to make the following:

3 red blocks	2 dark yellow blocks	1 light blue block
2 dark pink blocks	1 light yellow block	1 turquoise block
2 light pink blocks	1 dark green block	1 light aqua block
1 coral block	2 light green blocks	3 dark purple blocks
3 orange blocks	2 dark blue blocks	

Otherwise, make as many blocks as you would like in the colors you prefer.

4. Arrange the blocks, referring to the quilt assembly diagram (page 105) or following your own design.

5. Assemble the quilt top. With right sides together, sew the blocks into rows. Press each row in alternating directions so the seams rest together when you sew the rows. Pin and sew the rows together. Press.

6. When the quilt top is assembled, sew a straight or zigzag stitch ⅛″ in from the outside edge of the quilt. This will prevent the seams from splitting during handling before it is quilted.

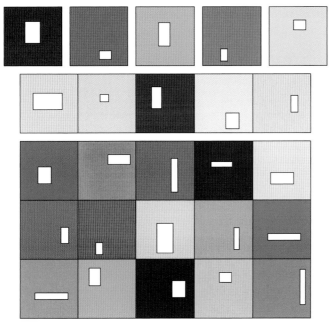

Quilt assembly diagram

BACKING, QUILTING, AND FINISHING

Refer to Turning the Pieced Top into a Quilt (pages 50–57) as needed.

1. Piece the backing fabric into a square at least 83″ × 83″. Press.

2. Layer the backing fabric, batting, and quilt top. Baste the quilt.

3. Quilt as desired.

4. Trim the excess batting and backing from the edge of the quilt.

5. Attach the binding by machine and stitch it down with your preferred method.

MAKE IT YOURS

- Arrange the blocks according to the rainbow. This is a more soothing visual effect.

- With blocks in a variety of values, arrange the quilt to emphasize the differences. Put lighter-value blocks in a single line or square.

- Instead of the rainbow effect, choose a handful of complementary colors and make up numerous blocks in various values and tones.

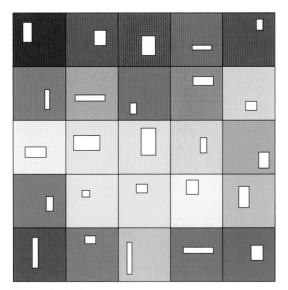

Arrange in rainbow.

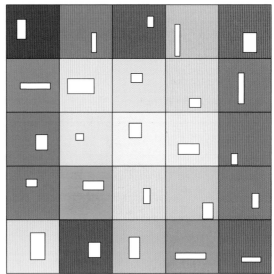

Emphasize differences in value.

ABOUT THE QUILTING

Each of the blocks was quilted individually, in a coordinating thread. The white blocks were outlined, and then the block was finished with a concentric squared-off pattern coming out from the white part. I used my walking foot. Work on the quilting from the center of the quilt out to minimize distortion.

Fortune Teller

Made by Cheryl Arkison

block size: 10″ × 10″

finished size: 60″ × 60″

It's no secret that I am drawn to bright colors. When I organized my scraps, however, I noticed that the neutrals section was overflowing. It was an unexpected surprise. Just seeing that bin was quite inspiring. Amanda Jean and I brainstormed for a bit and came up with this design together.

When folded to show off the contrasting corners, it reminded me of a childhood game. Folded paper with some carefully written predictions, combined with the curiosity of elementary school kids, makes for a silly fortune teller game. My prediction? You'll love making this easy quilt.

MATERIALS

- Scraps varying in size from snippets to strings/strips to sections, in 5 colors

- Backing: 4 yards

- Batting: 68″ × 68″

- Binding: ¼ yard or 2 strips 3″ × width of fabric to match each color used for blocks

CUTTING

Binding:

Cut 2 strips of each color 2½″ × width of fabric for 8 binding strips.

ABOUT FABRIC SELECTION

Of course you don't have to do a neutral quilt with this design. Pick any four colors and a neutral or five favorite colors to make the blocks. Don't pick more than that, however, unless you want to create additional large color blocks—for example, in a 2 × 6 or 3 × 3 large block layout.

Make This Quilt

QUILT TOP

Refer to Quilt Construction Basics (pages 41–58) as needed.

1. Sort the scraps into individual color piles. Don't worry about the size or shape.

2. Make slabs (page 48) in the following sizes:

   4 white 10½″ × 10½″

   8 in each of the 4 remaining colors, all 10½″ × 10½″

You should have 36 blocks in all.

3. Arrange the blocks in 4 sets of nine-patches. The white block should be centered in the nine-patch.

4. With right sides together, sew the 9 blocks together for each large nine-patch block. Sew as you would any other nine-patch—make 3 rows each with 3 blocks; then sew the rows together. Press the seams so they nest.

5. With right sides together, sew the top nine-patches together; then sew the bottom nine-patches together. Press the seams in alternate directions so they nest when sewn together. Sew the top half to the bottom half. Press.

6. When the quilt top is assembled, sew a straight or zigzag stitch ⅛" in from the outside edge of the quilt. This will prevent the seams from splitting during handling.

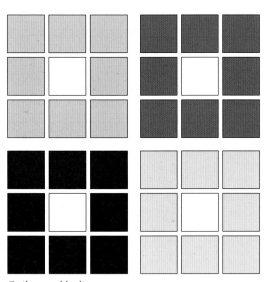

Quilt assembly diagram

BACKING, QUILTING, AND FINISHING

Refer to Turning the Pieced Top into a Quilt (pages 50–57) as needed.

1. Piece the backing fabric into a square at least 68" × 68". Press.

2. Layer the backing fabric, batting, and quilt top. Baste the quilt.

3. Quilt as desired.

4. Trim the excess batting and backing from the edge of the quilt.

5. The pictured quilt has binding that matches the blocks. If this isn't a concern to you, bind the quilt in your preferred manner. Otherwise, follow the directions below.

Pieced binding

1. With right sides together, sew pairs of binding strips together with a straight seam, matching the color combinations in the quilt. Refer to the quilt photo (page 109).

2. Fold the binding strips in half along the length, wrong sides together, and press well. This creates a double-fold binding.

3. Following the instructions in Binding Method 2 (page 56), pin and sew the binding to the sides of the quilt, matching the seam in the binding to the seam in the quilt.

ABOUT THE QUILTING

Whenever you are quilting slab quilts, and particularly this one, you should keep the quilting simple. It is very easy to skip stitches with the constant movement through multiple layers on slab projects when free-motion quilting. If you are a beginning free-motion quilter, this is something to keep in mind. If you are an experienced quilter, make sure you know how to manage this potential. That's why I went for straight-line quilting on this one. I secured the quilt first with stitching between the four main color blocks. Then I chose a free-form diagonal pattern, changing the thread for each quadrant. Just to be different, of course, I quilted the white blocks with a concentric square pattern.

MAKE IT YOURS

* Focus on values and tones in a single colorway to make the blocks. This would require more scraps, but it would be a fantastic challenge and a great lesson on choosing fabrics.

* Adapt the design to make it larger or smaller depending on the size of blocks that you make.

* Not interested in piecing slabs? Use pre-cuts, sorted by color (mix up lines if you have to), to achieve the same effect. You could also cut squares from your stash.

Leaves and Vine

Pieced by Cheryl Arkison
Quilted by Amanda Jean Nyberg

finished size: 48″ × 36″

MATERIALS

- Range of scraps—including snippets, strings, strips, and sections—of single color and similar value

- Brown: 1 strip 4″ × width of fabric for vine

- Dark reds, pinks, purples, and oranges: scraps at least 4″ × 4″ for leaves

- Backing: 2½ yards

- Batting: 56″ × 48″

- Binding: ½ yard

- Fusible web (if you prefer to fuse) 17″ wide: ⅔ yard

CUTTING

Binding:

Cut 5 strips 2½″ × width of fabric.

I always kept a set of markers in my day-job office for the moments when an image, an inspiration, or a quilt popped into my head. This one started out as a simple line drawing of the vine and leaves on a green square. In my head I pictured a single background. But when I started working on slabs, I knew that's how this quilt would come to be.

The appliqué is done by hand, as is a good portion of the quilting. Those little leaves were begging for a hand touch. You could also, quite easily, simply fuse the appliqué and finish with either a satin stitch or with outline quilting lines.

ABOUT FABRIC SELECTION

Central to this design is the high contrast between the background fabrics and the appliqué. There are two factors to success on this front. One, aim for scraps with similar values when making the slab; stick with light and medium-value fabrics that are more light than dark. And two, pick dark, bright fabrics for the appliqué.

Make This Quilt

PREPARING THE APPLIQUÉ

Note: If you are using fusible web, iron the web to the back side of the fabric before tracing and cutting.

1. Trace the vine template pattern* 1 (page 116) on the paper side of the freezer paper. Join as many templates as needed along the join lines to create the required length. Cut out the vine on the traced line. Iron, shiny side down, onto the right side of the vine fabric. For hand appliqué, cut out the vine allowing an extra ⅛″–¼″ for the turn-under allowance. For fusible appliqué, cut out at the edge of the freezer paper.

2. Trace the leaf template patterns* 2–5 (page 116) on the paper side of the freezer paper. Cut out a variety of leaves from the dark red, pink, purple, and orange scraps. For hand appliqué, include an extra ⅛″–¼″ around the edge for the turn-under allowance. For fusible appliqué, cut out at the edge of the freezer paper.

If you prefer, you can cut out the vine and leaves freehand.

QUILT TOP

Refer to Quilt Construction Basics (pages 41–58) as needed.

1. Make slabs (page 48) in the following sizes:

3 squares 15½″ × 15½″; label A, B, and U

3 squares 12½″ × 12½″; label C, D, and M

4 squares 9½″ × 9½″; label G, I, J, and T

3 squares 6½″ × 6½″; label K, L, and S

1 square 3½″ × 3½″; label P

1 rectangle 6½″ × 9½″; label F

2 rectangles 3½″ × 9½″; label H and N

4 rectangles 3½″ × 6½″; label E, O, Q, and R

Alternatively, you could make the slabs into 12 squares 12½″ × 12½″. We prefer the more random look created by the puzzle approach, but that isn't the only way to do it.

2. Assemble the quilt top. If you followed our approach, refer to the quilt assembly diagram (next page) and the sewing order below. Otherwise, arrange blocks in a 4 × 3 block layout. With right sides together, sew the 12½″ × 12½″ blocks into rows; then sew the rows together. For either sewing process, press each seam as you sew.

With right sides together:

Sew A to B.

Sew C to D.

Sew E to F.

Sew CD to EF.

Sew G to H to I to J.

Sew AB to CDEF to GHIJ.

Sew K to L.

Sew KL to M.

Sew N to O to P to Q.

Sew R to S.

Sew RS to T.

Sew RST to U.

Sew NOPQ to RSTU.

Sew NOPQRSTU to KLM.

With right sides together, sew the 2 sections together. Press.

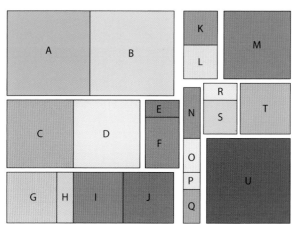

Quilt assembly diagram

3. When the quilt top is assembled, sew a straight or zigzag stitch ⅛″ in from the outside edge of the quilt. This will prevent the seams from splitting during handling until it is quilted.

4. Pin, baste, or glue the vine appliqué on the background. Refer to the quilt photo (page 113) for placement. Make sure the vine is flat and smooth. Appliqué using your preferred method.

5. Arrange all the leaves and baste before you stitch them down. Appliqué the leaves next to the vine, using your preferred method.

BACKING, QUILTING, AND FINISHING

Refer to Turning the Pieced Top into a Quilt (pages 50–57) as needed.

1. Piece the backing fabric to a rectangle 56″ × 44″.

2. Layer the backing fabric, batting, and quilt top. Baste the quilt.

3. Quilt the background first; then quilt the appliqué.

4. Trim the excess batting and backing from the edge of the quilt.

5. Attach the binding by machine and stitch it down with your preferred method.

MAKE IT YOURS

This quilt works in an infinite number of colorways. Try one of the following:

- White or cream background with brights, spring colors, or autumnal colors
- Blue background with whites and yellows
- Black background with brights

Increase the size of the quilt by making the background bigger and adding to the number of appliqué pieces used.

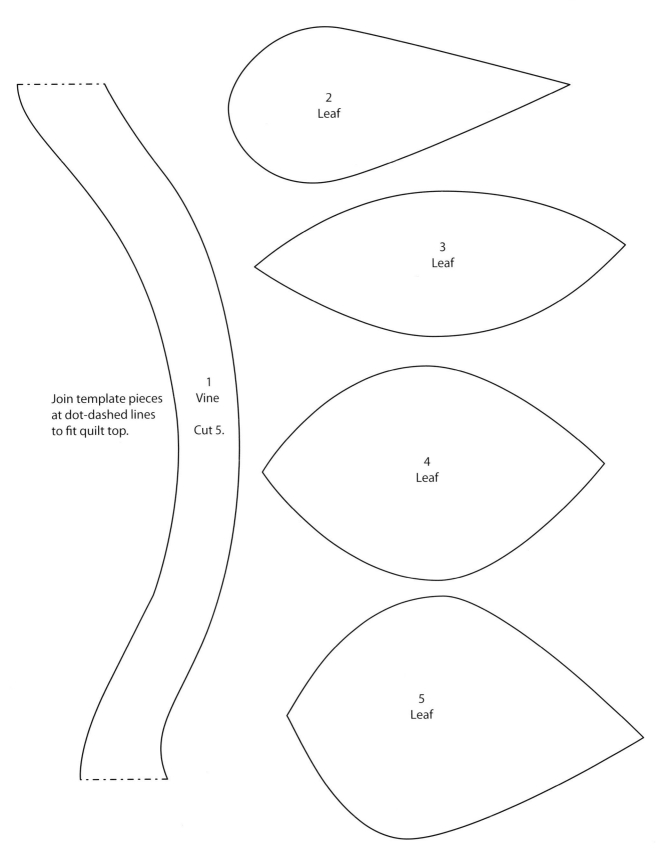

2
Leaf

3
Leaf

1
Vine

Cut 5.

Join template pieces
at dot-dashed lines
to fit quilt top.

4
Leaf

5
Leaf

ABOUT THE QUILTING

Amanda Jean quilted this one after Cheryl pieced the slab and completed the appliqué. The background is quilted with free-motion loops in green, to provide texture. We didn't want the background to pop. Instead, the appliqué is high-lighted with some hand quilting.

High Five

Made by Amanda Jean Nyberg

block size: 4½″ × 4½″ and 9″ × 9″

finished size: 63″ × 90″

The motivation behind this quilt was simple—to play with color and to empty the scrap bins. This is another quilt that uses 100 percent scraps and no filler (sashing or background). This was a fun quilt to make because it combines so many fabrics from previous projects, and it allowed me to play with all the colors of my scrap bins. I also enjoyed mixing two different block sizes into one quilt.

MATERIALS

- A variety of strings, snippets, and larger scraps for blocks
- Backing: 5½ yards
- Batting: 71″ × 98″
- Binding: ¾ yard

CUTTING

Binding:

Cut 8 strips 2½″ × width of fabric.

ABOUT FABRIC SELECTION

For the small blocks: Think about contrast when making these. Use four similarly colored strings for the outside and a contrasting-color center. Multicolored fabrics or small fussy-cut pieces work great for the centers.

For the large blocks: Use a monochromatic color scheme throughout the block, with an inner white border to separate the middle square and the border.

Make This Quilt

QUILT TOP

Refer to Quilt Construction Basics (pages 41–58) as needed.

1. For the small blocks, start with a snippet 1½"–2", square or rectangular in shape. Sew another snippet or string to the first, right sides together. Press, and trim off any overhanging ends. Add 3 more strips, Log Cabin–style, around the center. Make sure the block will measure at least 5" × 5" when you are done adding strips. Trim the block to 5" × 5".

2. Repeat to make 260 small blocks in a variety of colors.

Make 260 small blocks.

3. For the large blocks, start with a scrap, 2½"–3" square or rectangular in shape. Take 2 white strips approximately 1½" wide and sew them to opposite sides of the center block. Press and trim. Add 2 more white strips approximately 1½" wide to the remaining sides. Press and trim.

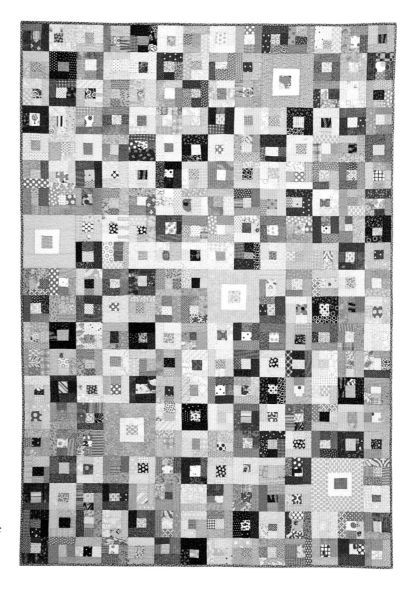

Add colored strips to the block as described in Step 1, using strips approximately 3″–4″ wide. Make sure the block is larger than 9½″ on all sides. Use the same fabric for all the colored strips if possible, or use 4 different fabrics with similar color and value. Trim the block to 9½″ × 9½″.

4. Repeat to make a total of 5 large blocks.

Make 5 large blocks.

5. Arrange the blocks according to the quilt assembly diagram.

6. Sew the blocks into rows. Press. In row pairs containing a large block, sew the 2 rows on either side of the large block, sew the rows together, and then sew to either side of the large block. Sew all the rows together to complete the quilt top. Press.

MAKE IT YOURS

- Vary the number of small and large blocks.

- Make the quilt using only large or only small blocks.

- Use a single color for all the centers throughout the quilt.

- Use a limited color palette to make a gradient design. For example, start with a variety of blue blocks at the top, add various blue/green blocks throughout the center of the quilt, and then place a variety of green blocks at the bottom of the quilt.

- Pair up four small blocks and alternate with a large block. Repeat that pattern throughout, like a checkerboard.

7. When the quilt top is assembled, sew a straight or zigzag stitch ⅛″ in from the outside edge of the quilt. This will prevent the seams from splitting during handling until it is quilted.

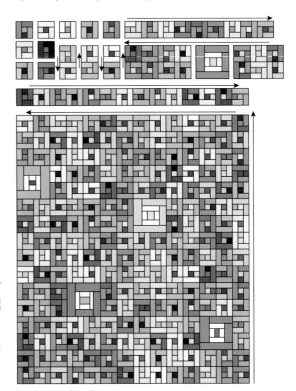

Quilt assembly diagram

BACKING, QUILTING, AND FINISHING

Refer to Turning the Pieced Top into a Quilt (pages 50–57) as needed.

1. Piece the backing fabric into a rectangle 71″ × 98″. Press.

2. Layer the backing fabric, batting, and quilt top. Baste the quilt.

3. Quilt as desired.

4. Trim the excess batting and backing from the edge of the quilt.

5. Attach the binding by machine and stitch it down with your preferred method.

ABOUT THE QUILTING

Because there is so much color in this quilt, when it came time to quilt it I kept things simple, because a detailed design would get lost. I simply stippled the entire quilt with a neutral-colored thread, which adds a great texture to the quilt.

Gumdrops

Made by Amanda Jean Nyberg

finished size: 39½″ × 55″

MATERIALS

- Variety of scraps:
  370–400 scraps
  approximately 2″ × 2″

- Background fabric: 2 yards

- Lite Steam-A-Seam 2:
  3 packages (5 sheets per
  package), or your preferred
  double-sided fusible web

- Binding: 46 rectangles
  2½″ × 5″

- Backing: 2¾ yards

- Batting: 48″ × 63″

Add some curves to your quilt! This is a fun way to use up some of the larger snippets you've got lying around. Don't be afraid of the curves—they are fused, an easy way to add them to any quilt for a relaxed look.

The gumdrops in this quilt are cut free form, but templates are provided if you prefer to use them. The fusible web used to attach the gumdrops adds some weight, so keep that in mind when choosing your batting. The binding uses even more scraps, including leftover binding strips from other projects.

ABOUT FABRIC SELECTION

Sometimes it is best to use a single background piece to tie a wide variety of scraps together. For the gumdrops, I limited the color scheme to warm colors—pinks, reds, oranges, and yellows. Adding the purples into the mix was Cheryl's idea. What a fun pop! All these scraps came from my scrap baskets, but never before have these fabrics played together in this color combination.

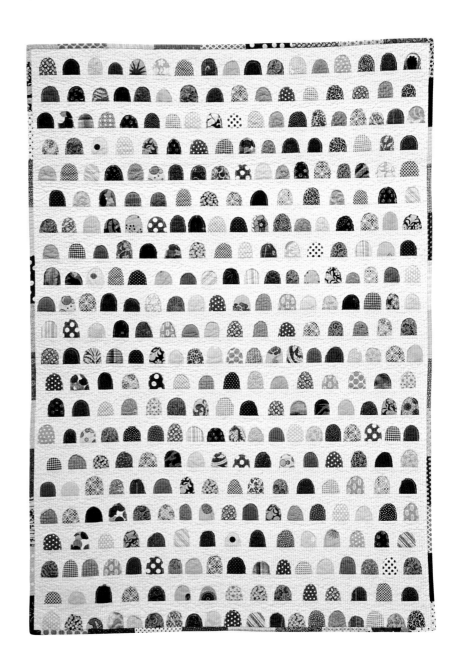

CUTTING

Fusible web:

Cut each sheet into 6 strips 2″ × 9″. Cut the strips into pieces 1¾″ wide. Each 9″ × 12″ sheet will yield 30 rectangles 1¾″ × 2″. You will need approximately 12½ sheets of fusible web, depending on how close together you place the gumdrops.

Save Time by Using a Paper Cutter

You can cut sheets of fusible web to the desired size efficiently with a paper cutter.

Scraps:

Fuse the interfacing rectangles to the back of the scraps. Cut out gumdrop shapes. Cut freehand or use the gumdrop template patterns 1–6 (page 126). Ensure a wide variety of shapes in your gumdrops. If using templates, make sure you use them all and cut a variety of each.

Save Time by Cutting Multiple Gumdrops at Once

It is easy to stack together fabric, and with scissors cut out the gumdrop shapes in multiples (up to 3).

Background:

Cut 22 strips 3″ × 40″.

Make This Quilt

QUILT TOP

*Refer to Quilt Construction Basics
(pages 41–58) as needed.*

1. Arrange the gumdrops on a strip of background fabric. The pictured quilt (page 123) has between 15 and 19 gumdrops per row. Align the flat edge of the gumdrop with the bottom edge of the fabric. Vary the distances between gumdrops and vary the colors of the gumdrops within each row. Fuse the gumdrops to the fabric according to the fusible web package instructions.

2. Repeat for all 22 rows.

3. Arrange the rows.

4. With right sides together, sew the rows together and press the seams away from the gumdrops.

5. When the quilt top is assembled, sew a straight or zigzag stitch ⅛″ in from the outside edge of the quilt. This will prevent the seams from splitting during handling until it is quilted.

Take a Digital Photo of the Quilt Top before Sewing the Rows Together

A photo allows you to see the quilt with a fresh set of eyes. If you notice any areas of concentrated color in the quilt top, rearrange the rows. It's better to check this out before sewing together the rows rather than after.

BACKING, QUILTING, AND FINISHING

*Refer to Turning the Pieced Top into a Quilt
(pages 50–57) as needed.*

1. Piece the backing fabric to a rectangle 48″ × 63″.

2. Layer the backing fabric, batting, and quilt top. Baste the quilt.

3. Use quilting stitches to outline the gumdrops and secure the shapes to the quilt. Quilt the rest of the quilt as desired.

4. Trim the excess batting and backing from the edge of the quilt.

5. To make the binding: With right sides together, sew the 2½″ × 5″ rectangles end to end, using straight seams. Iron the seams open to reduce bulk. Fold the strip in half lengthwise and press well.

6. Attach the binding by machine; stitch it down with your preferred method.

MAKE IT YOURS

- Use a gray background and a variety of blue, green, and aqua solids for the gumdrops.

- Use only black and white fabrics for the gumdrops, with a brightly colored background, such as lime green.

- Turn every other row upside down.

- Vary the heights of some of the background strips. Adjust the heights of the gumdrops accordingly or leave the extra space over the gumdrops empty.

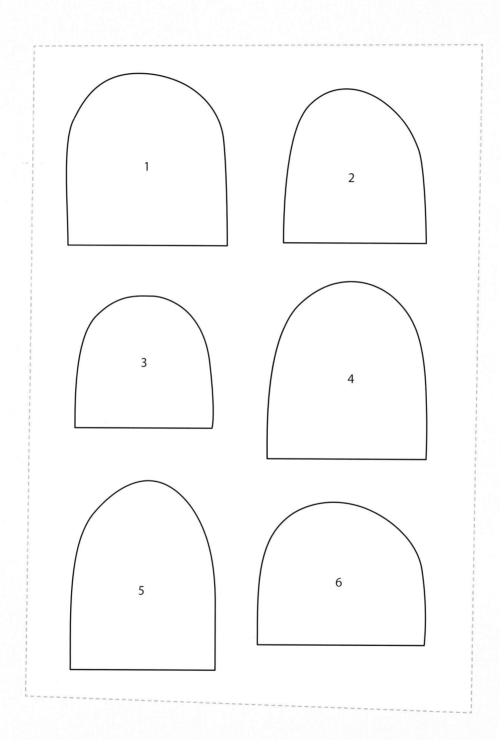

ABOUT THE QUILTING

First, I used a walking foot to quilt straight lines directly under the rows of gumdrops. This stabilized the quilt and allowed for easier free-motion quilting. Next, I outlined the gumdrops using a free-motion foot. I went back and forth over the edges of each gumdrop, for a total of three stitching lines. This can be very free form. After all the gumdrops were outlined, I quilted swirls in the white background sections. This helped keep the background flat and makes the gumdrops pop even more.

Checkerboard

Made by Amanda Jean Nyberg

finished size: 80″ × 88″

MATERIALS

- Whites, creams, and bright colors: scraps, at least 2½″ × 2½″

- Backing: 5½ yards

- Batting: 88″ × 96″

- Binding: ¾ yard

CUTTING

Whites and creams:

Cut 880 squares 2½″ × 2½″.

Various colors:

Cut 880 squares 2½″ × 2½″.

Binding:

Cut 9 strips 2½″ × width of fabric.

When I first started making quilts, I was stuck on "just plain squares" for a long time. In fact, my quilt mentor used to tease me about it. The reason that I can't get enough of this type of quilt is because you can create a completely different look by changing the combination of fabrics. This is a straightforward quilt pattern made from one simple shape, but the sheer number of squares and the color placement are what make it special. It's a good place to use up those small bits of fabric left over from all your previous projects.

This quilt isn't a weekend project. It will be much more enjoyable if you make a row here and there. This type of quilt can become a "scrapbook" of sorts of past projects. The 2½″ squares are easy to come by, and this is a perfect way to use them up.

ABOUT FABRIC SELECTION

The fabrics in this quilt fall into two categories: whites/creams and colors. For the whites and creams I used a number of different shades. I didn't want to buy yardage of a single background color to make a scrappy quilt, so working with twenty different whites from the scrap basket was my solution. It wasn't my first thought, but it's the "make do with what you have" mentality that makes this quilt what it is.

When picking the colors, I tried to avoid low-volume fabrics. Instead I picked bright, saturated, or busy prints. A few light fabrics were used, but sparingly. I wanted a defined checkerboard pattern to emerge. The more prints in this quilt, the better. Because the blocks are small, even some ugly fabrics can sneak their way into the quilt and feel right at home.

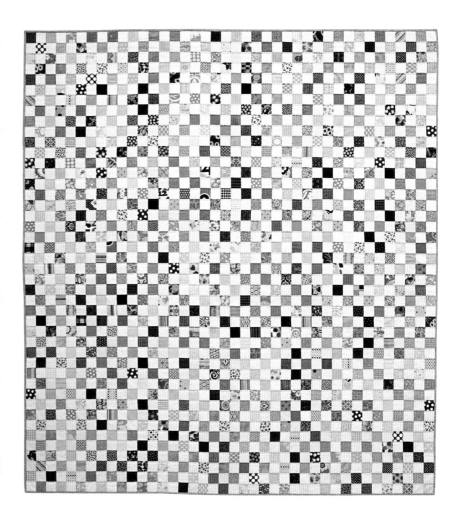

Make This Quilt

QUILT TOP

Refer to Quilt Construction Basics (pages 41–58) as needed.

1. With right sides together, sew 40 squares end to end. Alternate colored blocks with white or cream blocks. Each row starts with a colored block and ends with a white or cream block. Make 44 rows.

Use a Paper Bag to Step into Improvisation

If you have a hard time piecing random scraps together, use the paper bag technique to help you break free. Place all the colored blocks in a paper bag. Place all the whites/creams in another paper bag. Grab 1 square from each bag, and sew the 2 squares together. Repeat this process 20 times. Sew those 20 pairs together until there are 40 squares, end to end. You will be surprised how beautifully it all works out.

2. Place a row on your ironing surface with a colored block on the left-hand side, and press all the seams to the right. Repeat this exact pressing direction for each row. It's important to press the seam allowances of every row in the same direction. Every other row will be rotated 180° and the seams on those rows will be reversed. This will allow the seams to nest and the checkerboard pattern will be formed.

3. Arrange the rows, rotating every other one, and number them to keep in order. Pin a scrap of paper with the number on it to the first block on the left-hand side of each row.

4. With right sides together, sew all the rows together and press well.

5. When the quilt top is assembled, sew a straight or zigzag stitch ⅛″ in from the outside edge of the quilt. This will prevent the seams from splitting during handling until it is quilted.

BACKING, QUILTING, AND FINISHING

Refer to Turning the Pieced Top into a Quilt (pages 50–57) as needed.

1. Piece the backing fabric into a rectangle 88″ × 96″. Press.

2. Layer the backing fabric, batting, and quilt top. Baste the quilt.

3. Quilt as desired.

4. Trim the excess batting and backing from the edge of the quilt.

5. Attach the binding by machine and stitch it down with your preferred method.

MAKE IT YOURS

- Limit the color palette to just reds and whites or just blues and whites.

- Use whites and creams paired with only warm colors—reds, oranges, pinks, and yellows.

- Use whites and creams paired with only cool colors—purples, greens, blues, and grays.

- Use a charcoal gray in place of the whites and creams.

- Make this quilt using a values treatment, alternating light prints with dark prints.

ABOUT THE QUILTING

I tried many different ways of quilting (on this quilt, no less!) before I settled on a design. After spending a lot of time picking out my stitches, I learned that sometimes keeping it simple is best. Using a walking foot, I echoed the block lines ¼″ to the left and ¼″ below each seamline.

Checkerboard

Up, Up, and Away

Made by Amanda Jean Nyberg

block size: 2″ × 2″

finished size: 42½″ × 53¾″

MATERIALS

- 589 triangles left over from 2½″ binding strips in various colors, or cut as described in Cutting (page 44)

- Background: 2¾ yards

- Backing: 3 yards

- Batting: 51″ × 62″

- Binding: ½ yard

- 2½″ × 2½″ square ruler for trimming triangles (*optional*)

This quilt was composed of the tiny triangles that are left over from joining the ends of binding strips as well as other triangle scraps I had on hand. I haven't always saved binding triangles. In fact, this is my first big project using them. Because the pieces are so small, even a baby quilt requires a lot of triangles. You may want to plan ahead and start saving now. Another option for the scraps would be to use 2½″ × 2½″ squares cut in half diagonally.

The blocks are set on point, which means that the quilt is assembled in rows on the diagonal. Instead of adding in setting triangles, the points are trimmed off after assembly. This allows the pattern of the quilt to go "off the page," so to speak.

ABOUT FABRIC SELECTION

Looking at this quilt, you can see that most of my binding selections from previous quilts lean toward bold, saturated colors. This is why it's perfect to pair the triangles with a white background—the colors of the triangles really stand out.

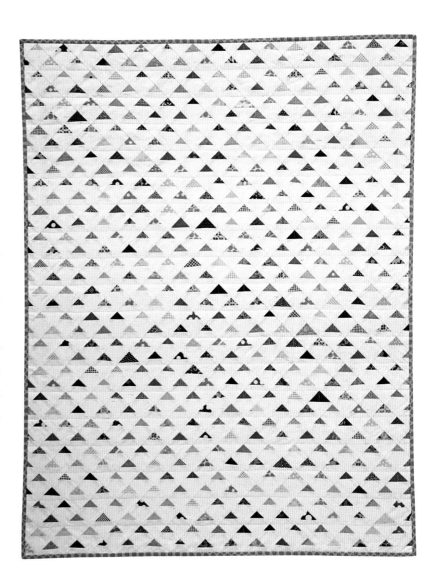

Make This Quilt

CUTTING

Triangles:

If you don't have triangles left over from binding strips, cut 295 squares 2½″ × 2½″ from assorted scraps; then cut each square on the diagonal.

Background:

Cut 38 strips 2½″ × width of fabric; then cut the strips into 605 squares 2½″ × 2½″.

Binding:

Cut 6 strips 2½″ × width of fabric.

QUILT TOP

Refer to Quilt Construction Basics (pages 41–58) as needed.

1. With right sides together, place a binding triangle on the corner of a background block as shown. Before sewing the triangle in place, fold it over the corner to make sure that when it is sewn and pressed it will cover the entire corner of the background block. Be sure to account for the seam allowance. Sew using a ¼″ seam allowance.

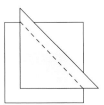

Place triangle on block and sew.

2. Fold the colored triangle over the white corner and press. If any of the white background fabric shows after you have sewn and ironed the triangle, it will need to be redone.

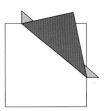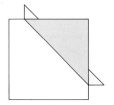

White background not covered; need to redo.

Corner of the white background completely covered.

When the placement of the triangle is correct, the corner of the white background is completely covered by the binding triangle.

3. Trim the white fabric behind the colored triangle, leaving a ¼″ seam allowance.

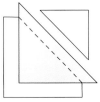

Trim.

4. Trim the block to 2½″ × 2½″ square. A 2½″ square ruler is helpful.

5. Repeat Steps 1–4 to make a total of 589 blocks.

6. Arrange the 16 remaining white 2½″ × 2½″ squares across the top of the quilt. These will be the top block of each diagonal row. Because the tips of these blocks will be trimmed off later, they do not need to be pieced.

7. Arrange the pieced blocks, referring to the quilt assembly diagram.

Quilt assembly diagram

8. With right sides together, sew the blocks into rows. Press all the seam allowances in a row in the same direction and alternate the pressing direction from row to row so the seams nest when the rows are sewn together.

9. With right sides together, sew the rows together. Press.

10. Using a rotary cutter and a long ruler, trim the excess triangles off the quilt. Work on a section at a time, moving the ruler as needed. Continue to trim until there is a straight edge around the perimeter of the quilt.

Trim edges of quilt.

11. When the quilt top is assembled, sew a straight or zigzag stitch ⅛″ in from the outside edge of the quilt. This will prevent the seams from splitting during handling until it is quilted.

BACKING, QUILTING, AND FINISHING

Refer to Turning the Pieced Top into a Quilt (pages 50–57) as needed.

1. Piece the backing fabric into a rectangle 51″ × 62″. Press.

2. Layer the backing fabric, batting, and quilt top. Baste the quilt.

3. Quilt as desired.

4. Trim the excess batting and backing from the edge of the quilt.

5. Attach the binding by machine and stitch it down with your preferred method.

MAKE IT YOURS

- Use a different-sized background block. A 4″ × 4″ block would cause the background to be more prominent. This would cause the triangles to float a bit more.

- Use a dark color, such as gray, for the background and use only white triangles.

- Use a black or gray background instead of white.

- Use a straight setting rather than an on-point setting to create a totally different look.

ABOUT THE QUILTING

Because of all the seams in this quilt, I knew I wanted to use a walking foot to quilt it. I used the blocks in the quilt top as my quilting guide so I wouldn't have to mark anything. I quilted simple straight lines, both horizontally and vertically, through every other block.

The Original Ticker Tape

Made by Amanda Jean Nyberg

finished size: 33½″ × 45½″

MATERIALS

- Assorted scraps in various sizes, most about 1″ × 2″ but none larger than 2½″ × 2½″

- Background: 1½ yards white fabric

- Backing (busy print is suggested): 1½ yards

- Batting: 42″ × 54″

- Binding: ⅓ yard

CUTTING

Background:

Cut 1 rectangle 34″ × 46″.

Backing:

Cut 1 rectangle 42″ × 54″.

Binding:

Cut 5 strips 2½″ × width of fabric.

The ticker tape quilt concept originated from my desire to use up as much of my fabric as possible, even down to scraps that are only 1″ × 1″ square. The fact that there was little room for seam allowances wasn't a deterrent. I simply quilted the tiny pieces onto a quilt sandwich and worked them together like a puzzle until the entire background was filled. The name of the quilt (which quite possibly is the best part) was the brainchild of my friend Susan. She had actually suggested "ticker tape" for another quilt I was working on at the time, but it suited this one perfectly, so I paired the two and the ticker tape quilt was born. This quilt will certainly have you thinking twice before throwing any scrap away!

ABOUT FABRIC SELECTION

Every color of the rainbow is represented in this quilt. The only fabrics to avoid are very light-colored fabrics that won't read well against the white background.

Make This Quilt

MAKE IT YOURS

- Use a background color, such as aqua, and add only cream and white snippets.

- Use a dark background (gray, brown, or black) instead of white.

- Use linen for the background to increase the textural quality of the quilt.

- Cut the snippets into circles instead of using rectangles and squares. Attach with a free-motion or darning foot.

QUILT TOP

Refer to Quilt Construction Basics (pages 41–58) as needed.

1. Make a quilt sandwich that consists of the white fabric on top, the batting in the middle, and the backing on the bottom.

2. Baste the quilt sandwich (page 52).

3. Put a walking foot on your sewing machine. Choose any fabric scrap and attach the scrap to the quilt sandwich by stitching around the edges. Be sure to leave an empty space ¾″ from all the edges of the quilt. This will allow room for binding the quilt later.

4. Continue sewing down scraps, working the pieces together like a puzzle.

5. Fill in the scraps until the white space is full.

> ### Dedicate a Spot for Ticker Tape Pieces
>
> I have a basket on my worktable that I have designated for small pieces (all measure less than 2½″ × 2½″). I collect them as I cut for other projects. I do very little additional cutting of the scraps when adding them to the quilt—I only trim a sliver here and there as needed and let the random sizes dictate the layout.

6. Trim any excess batting and backing from the edge of the quilt.

7. Attach the binding by machine and stitch it down with your preferred method.

ABOUT THE QUILTING

All the scraps were attached with white thread. There are many starting and stopping points in the quilt, so choose the backing fabric with thread color in mind. A busy print that matches the thread color is ideal. The unique construction used for this quilt combines quilting and piecing all in one step. Keep in mind that when you wash the quilt, the ticker tape pieces will fray.

About the Authors

CHERYL ARKISON

 You've come a long way, baby! It's a cliché for sure, but an apt description of Cheryl's journey from sewing tube dresses for her dolls to her first quilt book. There were stops at her grandmother's house for lessons on cross-stitch that never quite took, the crowning achievement of winning the grade 8 Home Ec Award, and those years cooking to put herself through school.

Her not-so-secret additional life goals are to be a DJ, live in a house with a porch, and learn how to juggle. As a mother, wife, daughter, friend, designer, writer, teacher, and scotch lover, she's managed the last one so far. Add to that her other side career as a food writer. See all her work (writing and quilting), inspiration, and challenges at cherylarkison.com.

Cheryl lives in Calgary, Alberta, with her husband, kids, and pooch.

AMANDA JEAN NYBERG

 Considering that she grew up in a family of six children, it comes as no surprise that Amanda Jean is frugal. It is in her blood, whether she likes it or not, and it's reflected in her quiltmaking. Using up every last bit of fabric has become one of the trademarks of her quilts. Given a choice between using scraps or stash, she would choose scraps nine times out of ten.

Amanda Jean can be found on the web at crazymomquilts.blogspot.com, which showcases the many ways she is living up to her blog name.

Amanda Jean, her husband, and their children live in Wisconsin. They love living in a place where the local parade offerings include not only candy but also cheese curds and chocolate milk.

stash BOOKS ®

fabric arts for a handmade lifestyle

If you're craving beautiful authenticity in a time of mass-production...Stash Books is for you. Stash Books is a line of how-to books celebrating fabric arts for a handmade lifestyle. Backed by C&T Publishing's solid reputation for quality, Stash Books will inspire you with contemporary designs, clear and simple instructions, and engaging photography.

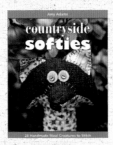

www.stashbooks.com